ELITE TO EVERYDAY
ATHLETE

9 Steps to Getting Off the SIDELINES of Life

ELITE TO EVERYDAY ATHLETE

9 STEPS TO GETTING OFF THE SIDELINES OF LIFE

EMILY COFFMAN

NEW DEGREE PRESS

COPYRIGHT © 2021 EMILY COFFMAN

ELITE TO EVERYDAY ATHLETE
9 Steps to Getting Off the SIDELINES of Life

ISBN   978-1-63676-490-0   *Paperback*
          978-1-63730-403-7   *Kindle Ebook*
          978-1-63730-404-4   *Ebook*

To my parents,

*Without you both, there wouldn't be
an athletic journey to write about.*

"It all comes with a catch. Because if your whole life was about building up to one race, one performance, or one event, how does that sustain everything that comes afterwards? Eventually, for me at least, there was one question that hit me like a ton of bricks: Who was I outside of the swimming pool?"

—MICHAEL PHELPS, TWENTY-EIGHT-
TIME OLYMPIC MEDAL SWIMMER

TABLE OF CONTENTS

———

9 Steps to Getting Off the S.I.D.E.L.I.N.E.S. of Life

	THE NEW UNKNOWN	
S	Slow Down	☐
I	Intuitively Eat	☐
D	Develop Body Acceptance	☐
	THE MESSY MIDDLE	
E	Explore Your Identity	☐
L	Love Your Workout	☐
I	Improve Nutrition Knowledge	☐
	BETTER DAYS AHEAD	
N	Nurture New Athletic Role	☐
E	Expand Your Comfort Zone	☐
S	Spark a New Interest	☐

INTRODUCTION

―――

"The past ten years have been such a whirlwind that I haven't really processed all that has happened, and sometimes I wonder whether I ever will."

—*ALY RAISMAN, SIX-TIME OLYMPIC MEDALIST INGYMNASTICS*

Like many athletes, I dedicated most of my childhood and young adult life to sports. After my last day of competition, I left sports ready to move on and never look back. I didn't have a bad athletic career, but I was eager to graduate from both college and sports and jump right into the next phase of my life.

I was ready for this change, but I wasn't ready for the feelings that came with it: those of frustration and loneliness from missing sports in my life. What I didn't realize was when I retired, I lost my identity. I lost my joy, a purpose in life, and my sense of self all in that one day. Yes, I was excited to have freedom of my time and endless possibilities for what was next, but I also felt myself falling deeper into a pit of hopeless-ness, wishing to get back the things I'd lost.

I thought these feelings would work like a light switch. After leaving sports my spark got switched off, and I felt lost. I thought the switch would light again as soon as the next thing came and I would be back to my old self. However, this was not the case. All I'd built ended in one day, and there was no quick fix to move on with my life.

I recently spoke with another former athlete, Millicent Sykes, about her transition out of ballet after high school, and she had very similar feelings to my own. She went through a period of grief and described it as "very unique and different than losing a pet, parent, or family member. I lost a piece of myself in a way, which is a very intimate and difficult process that takes a while."

> All I'd built ended in one day, and there was no quick fix to move on with my life.

After ballet, she never found anything that ful-filled her the same way dancing did. She tried a lot of different activities, but they were all a distraction from what she was actually missing. Millicent wasn't looking for something to fill her time. She was looking for something she could feel passionate about again. She tried new sports, clubs, and other interests, but it wasn't until she took a psychology course in school that she "felt jazzed again, a lot of the fire was fueled."

Studying psychology was never going to fulfill her in the exact way ballet had done. It wasn't going to be a physical activity, community, hobby, and identity. But it was her new passion. Just a few years after retiring from sports, she told me, "When

I graduated, I felt the similar passion that I had when I was dancing ballet, now with the idea of becoming a sports psychologist. So, it was a transfer of passions in a way." Sure, psychology was a new passion, but dance was a passion and so much more. It was her entire life. Unfortunately, it's not always easy to fill gaps like these.

Many athletes have common struggles after the game is over—loneliness and the lack of coaching, support, or competition—and it's normal to try to find something new to replace the entire sport. Millicent found a different approach. She took steps to rebuild her life instead of using new things to try to distract herself and replace ballet. She stumbled on this method by chance, and I wondered if she was unique or if this was something from which all athletes could benefit. What I found has changed the way I see the future for former athletes.

RETIREMENT:

Most people think that once athletes leave their sport, they are blessed with freedom and flexibility and will "figure it out" from there. I believe differently. I think athletes enter athletic retirement with skewed ideas on healthy exercise routines and eating patterns. Combine these with the big life change of losing your passion and identity, and these issues only worsen.

The National Eating Disorders Association estimates that disordered eating affects 62 percent of female athletes and 33 percent of male athletes. If an athlete doesn't have a solid understanding of nutrition while competing in sports, it's unlikely they will learn later while dealing with retirement. According to another study conducted on students and alumni of the University of Southern California, athletes average fifteen hours a week of exercise. Comparatively, both former college athletes and non-athletes average five hours a week of exercise. They conclude that "being a former college athlete has nothing to do with being a healthy exerciser."

The issue isn't that athletes have eating and exercise problems and this is why they have a tough transition. This issue is we never acknowledge the psychology behind the transition and how it affects an athlete's mental, emotional, and physical health. Instead, we assume that athletes are hardworking and value their bodies, so they'll just continue doing so.

I think the whole process of athletic retirement is sugarcoated.

At some point, everyone must retire from their sport. Huge changes occur in an athlete's life when this happens. Athletes are used to training for competition, not exercising because "it's good for you." Athletes know how to fuel their bodies for performance, not for desk job activity levels. Switching the focus from championships to day-to-day life isn't something that comes naturally and unfortunately leaves many in an all-or-nothing mindset.

But this isn't to say that retirement means athletes must completely start over. I believe that former athletes can use their skills for life after sports. The transition isn't like a light switch you turn on or off, and it's also not the end of a book that you've finished writing and will put away. Being an athlete is an experience that can help shape your future. You just have to learn to turn into an everyday athlete.

I felt compelled to write this because I think the whole process of athletic retirement is sugarcoated. Schools tell you that after graduation every company wants to hire athletes, and you compare yourself to older teammates that seem to be doing well in the real world. But there's so much more to life after sports than your career and success. What does it take to live a healthy life that makes you happy?

MY SAME STRUGGLE:

I felt this same struggle when I retired from rowing. I was a Division I athlete at the University of Oklahoma, something for which I was really proud. Spring break of my senior year, while most college students were at the beach partying, I was at the Olympic Training Center in Chula Vista, California. While my college friends were securing jobs and having their last drunken week at the beach, I was rowing. Every morning. Every evening. Every meal I was surrounded by athletes. Every conversation I had was with teammates. In our free time, the only place we went was our dorm room or back to the boathouse. I was completely consumed with my sport, my weight, and winning our upcoming championship.

After our training camp and the end of the season, my future in rowing did not look bright, and I realized I had achieved my goal just by training there. I had come to California burnt out but excited about training at one of the most elite centers in the world. Unfortunately, no amount of San Diego sun would convince me to stay. I left knowing that rowing was no longer the future for me.

> I never envisioned what would happen to me after my sports career ended.

That was March of my senior year. Two months later I graduated, never to compete again.

What was the future for me? After living out my childhood dream for four years and always striving for my next athletic goal, I realized I had never envisioned what would happen to me after my sports career ended. I felt I was behind my peers in getting a job. I hadn't had a single internship, never gained work experience, or even participated in a job interview. I knew about some of the expected difficulties for recent graduates like moving across the country, applying for full-time work, and saying goodbye to college friends. I anticipated these challenges. What I didn't expect was how much I struggled with my relationship with food and exercise and the perpetual feeling I held of being burnt out.

I thought being done with rowing would open a fun, new phase in my life, but there were a lot of hardships that came with it. To go from day-long rowing at one of the highest levels possible to retired is a change for which I thought I was ready. No one telling you how to train. No coaches checking up on you. No measurement to tell you whether or not you were succeeding. Yes, that sounded freeing and exciting, but I was filled with so much confusion. The changes in my physical, mental, and emotional health left me with so many questions. Is it normal to be gaining this weight? How can I still work out four hours a day with a nine-to-five job? Who am I supposed to be with this lack of structure and routine?

I discovered that even though I knew how to live a healthy life and thrive as an athlete, this didn't translate the same way in real life. I knew how to push my body to wake up at the ass crack of dawn, and I knew how to stay full enough for a five-hour practice, and I was able to focus myself on a goal. But I didn't know what counted as exercise when I was no longer training for anything. I didn't know how to create goals for myself moving forward.

"People know they want to change—know they need to change—but they resist, even to their own detriment,"

Psychologist Scott Bea, PsyD. concluded in an interview with Cleveland Clinic.

I knew for a while that I had to grow from my athletic identity, but for the longest time I didn't know how to do so. I've now learned how to have a healthy relationship with food and exercise by both trial and error and by learning from the experts. My goal is for you to know that you don't have to figure it out on your own. You can take steps to set yourself up for a smoother transition and get off the S.I.D.E.L.I.N.E.S. of life. It still won't be easy and won't come without trials, but you can give yourself a plan and a little bit of structure just like sports did for you for so many years. This book will be filled with interviews from former athletes who were in your position along with insights from dietitians, physical therapists, coaches, and more.

If you are an athlete of any level, or help support one, keep reading. The transition out of sports isn't as simple as creating a new schedule and setting a new goal. It goes deeper than that. Before we jump into the physical changes, we need to look at the mental health and psychology shifts that occur when someone retires from competitive sports. Let's be proactive in understanding how athletes can build healthy, happy, and successful post-sport lives.

THE NEXT HURDLE

"Imagine hitting your peak years in your late twenties, retiring in your thirties, and then going about the next half century trying to find a comparable experience."

—JON WERTHEIM, SPORTS ILLUSTRATED JOURNALIST

Rowing is a morning sport. I'm not a morning person. But regardless, I set my alarm every morning for 4:45 a.m., the bus left for the boathouse at 5:00 a.m., and I spent every morning of my college career watching the sun rise. I used to exert more energy every day before 8:00 a.m. than it took to write this book (okay, that might only be a slight exaggeration).

When the competition season ended and I traveled back home, I felt like a weight had been lifted off my shoulders. I immediately deleted all my alarms, took the most exciting grocery trip of my life (think mostly desserts), and prepared for the sweet feeling of what others call "a typical Friday night." It was time to catch up on the late nights and sleeping in that I had missed out on in college.

Unfortunately, this excitement was short-lived. I was still the ambitious athlete I used to be, but I had nowhere to put that ambition. Everything around me seemed like it wasn't enough. I used to have dreams of making it to the Olympics. I wanted to make a name for myself and be one of the best athletes ever. When those dreams faded and that lifeblood ended, I was left feeling like I was no longer special or talented. Everything I prided myself on was rooted in my athletic accomplishments, and I thought that sports might be the only thing in which I would ever thrive. I couldn't find anywhere else to replicate that same worthiness, that same purpose that sports and rowing gave me.

I was a coxswain for seven years. The coxswain is the small person at the back of the rowing boat who steers and instructs the rowers. I spent seven years trying to be the best coxswain I could be and spent even more time before that trying to be the best athlete. I spent so much time and energy for my performance and made many sacrifices. Then, just like that, it all ended. It was hard to have all my effort disappear overnight. I built my athletic skills for years just to have those efforts fail to translate into anything else.

I felt like I no longer knew my role in society, and I was wandering. I kept looking to outside standards of, "Maybe if I make enough money, then I'll feel worthy in society again. Maybe if I'm attractive and fit enough. Maybe if I contribute enough to create something great, then I'll feel worthy again." I kept trying to find something that could replace everything that athletics was in my world. It got to the point where the things I did have in my life—my relationships and my job—didn't seem like enough either. Yes, I had a steady job, but I wasn't a top performer there. Yes, I was in a loving relationship, but that didn't measure up to people cheering me on from the sidelines as I suited up to race every weekend.

So, what exactly was happening? I was feeling the lingering effects of burnout. Burnout can look like brain fog, numbness, or exhaustion, and it's one of the contributing factors that affects an athlete's mental state during this transition. I found the other most influential factors are injury, grief, and the need for reinvention. The psychology and emotions behind transitioning out of sports are crucial for an athlete to understand so they can be proactive if these feelings come up for them.

BURNOUT:

The author of *Foundations of Sport and Exercise Psychology*, Daniel Gould, defines burnout as "a physical, emotional, and social withdrawal from a formerly enjoyable sports activity. This withdrawal is characterized by emotional and physical exhaustion, reduced sense of accomplishments, and sport devaluation."

I left rowing absolutely exhausted. Sports are demanding, and athletes follow a rigorous schedule. Even if this seems like "part of the job," this mentality can really take a toll on an athlete. I thought burnout just meant not enjoying the sport anymore. I didn't realize how it could seep into all areas of my life.

The issue with burnout isn't that sports are no longer fun or that there are some aspects that feel more like a job than a fun hobby. The issue is the emotional toll that burnout takes on athletes. After retirement, an athlete should be able to look back at his or her career with a sense of accomplishment, no matter what the records show. All athletes can feel a sense of pride from dedicating themselves fully to an activity, working with others toward a common goal, and managing the discipline athletics builds.

Instead, when pushing through burnout, athletes no longer have this sense of accomplishment. In fact, they feel the opposite. Burnout is associated with feelings of low personal accomplishment, low self-esteem, failure, and depression. These feelings can skew how an athlete looks at their past and their future.

> I couldn't find anywhere else to replicate that same worthiness.

I had the pleasure to speak with Kelly Garrison-Funderburk, a 1988 Olympic gymnast. She felt burnout after competing in the Summer Olympics in South Korea. She came back to the United States to finish up her last year of college at the University of Oklahoma and she said, "I was done. I was burnt out. I was physically done. I was mentally done. I'd achieved my goal."

She achieved her goal of going to the Olympics, but it came at the cost of burnout. Kelly decided to quit gymnastics completely and didn't return to her college team the next season. Leaving the team meant that she lost her athletic scholarship, so she dropped out of school too. Burnout doesn't just affect how athletes feel about their sport. It affects how they feel about the rest of their life, too. Kelly recalled, "At the time, there were so many other issues I was going through. There were times where I was so depressed, I didn't care. It wasn't until much later that I went back to college and got my degree."

INJURY:

On the other hand, sometimes retirement can come by surprise. A large majority of athletes experience injuries, and over time, some can become career-ending. Daniel Gould stated, "Not only is being injured a significant life event, but it is one that happens quite often. It is estimated that over twenty-five million people are injured each year in the United States in sport, exercise, and recreational settings." Injuries are a common occurrence but often aren't addressed until after they happen.

Injuries are tough for athletes to work through, both physically and mentally. Boston Red Sox Second Baseman Dustin Pedroia was recently forced to retire due to recurring injuries. After many issues he had to get a partial knee replacement which left him retired from the sport for good. He said in an interview with reporters after announcing his retirement, "I'm glad none of you guys got a chance to see me (last year). I wasn't in a good place. I grinded every day just to be able to play with my kids and live a normal life." After his injury, Dustin wasn't trying to become an athlete again, he was just trying to live normally without pain. Living with lingering pain or fear of re-injury affects the mental state of former athletes.

Daniel Gould also found that the stress from injuries goes beyond just the pain. He wrote: "Interestingly, the

> The issue is the emotional toll that burnout takes on athletes.

greatest sources of stress were not the result of the physical aspects of the injuries. Rather, the psychological reactions (e.g., fear of re-injury, feeling that hopes and dreams were shattered, watching others get to perform) and social concerns (e.g., lack of attention, isolation, negative relationships) were mentioned more often as stressors." Sometimes the mental impact can be harder to navigate than the physical one. The rest of this book explores how to handle both.

REINVENTION:

No matter the reason for an athlete's athletic retirement, the transition is different than any other type of retirement. An athlete's career, 99 percent of the time, is not their final career. There are not many industries where someone would spend years training to be the best accountant, lawyer, or doctor just to be told that their career could no longer advance.

Richie Crowley, a former Brown University hockey player, moved to Europe to play professionally after college. He recalled having to move on to start something new after leaving hockey: "The moment I stopped playing hockey, I was just an entry-level employee at a Boston tech company like everyone else. I was so much less interesting to family, friends, and people I would meet. It was easy to impress a girl when I could say I was a professional athlete in Europe; but when I was an intern living with my parents—not so much."

After no longer having the title of professional athlete, he lost a lot of his confidence. Richie, like many athletes, left sports feeling like an expert at his game, only to have to find something new to learn. He recalled, "The way I saw myself was really impacted. I had to stop caring and be able to see myself for who I am, not how others saw me. That took a couple years of feeling forgotten, unimportant, and like I was nothing."

It's hard for athletes to feel like they must start over and reinvent themselves. Going through this transition in young adulthood can make former athletes feel like the dedication they put towards sport was all for nothing. Jeremiah Brown, a silver medal Olympian in rowing, spoke about this same idea in his interview for the book *Personal Next*. He said, "Although massive amounts of time and energy in becoming a professional in one's field are normally associated with ongoing returns, Olympians have mere days of peak performance."

Even if an athlete knows their end date is coming up, it's still hard to process. Acknowledging that athletic retirement is a unique

Sometimes the mental impact can be harder to navigate than the physical one.

transition and can look more like a reinvention can help athletes know that it's something they can work through slowly.

GRIEF:

The emotional aspect that athletes and outsiders alike tend to overlook is the amount of loss that comes from athletic retirement.

Loss looks different for everyone. It can be a loss of structure, goals, and routine. It can be a loss of enjoyment, their hobby, teammates, and a sense of winning. It can be a community loss of an athlete's support system, mentor, and coaches. It can be their loss of identity in worth, purpose, and joy. Regardless of the type of loss, grief is expected to follow.

Athletes have difficulty addressing these issues because they don't recognize them. Since the transition out of sports is not commonly talked about, an athlete might not realize how large of a toll it takes. They might think these emotions will pass and not try to address them. Sometimes just knowing what is going on makes a harsh emotion feel better. Knowing that it's normal to experience these feelings reminds you that you're not alone. During this time, it might be beneficial to talk to old coaches, former teammates, current friends, family, or a professional.

Even though athletes might leave sports for many reasons, there's one thing their retirement has in common: it's a complicated physical, mental, and emotional transition. The most important thing athletes can do during this time is put themselves first. In a period of large changes and confusing emotions, it's okay to take some time to prioritize yourself. This can feel selfish since many athletes have an engrained "team comes first" mentality, but it's crucial to a smooth transition.

This isn't to say that all parts of the transition are hard. There are many parts that a former athlete will enjoy about the next phase of life. But I want to talk about the parts that might come as unexpected roadblocks. The rest of this book will serve as a guide on how to understand what's happening to a former athlete's psychology and then how to start improving their physical health and mindset. The goal isn't to jump into the next exciting activity and look for where the grass is greener. The goal is to improve an athlete's life and outlook for where they're at now. Let's get started into phase one of the transition: the new unknown.

* * *

To hear more about my journey with burnout and overcoming it, listen to my podcast episode "Life After Sport . . . Now What?" at: http://emilycoffman.org/life-after-sport-now-what/

PHASE ONE: THE NEW UNKNOWN

CHAPTER 1:

THE NEVER-ENDING OFF SEASON

———

"After taking a month off from all exercise and transitioning to a corporate job in New York City, I began questioning my self-worth on an hourly basis. My corporate desk job just didn't give me the same high as slamming down a weight or sprinting through the line.

—*HILARY LEMONICK, DIVISION I LACROSSE*

What is athletic retirement? It's an off-season without a return date. Just like the beginning of any other off-season, this is the time to relax and recover. Most athletes retire at the end of a season. At this point the competition has reached its peak intensity, other areas of an athlete's life have been placed on the back burner, and their energy level is running on empty. The athlete's body is tired from being pushed seven days a week, and their emotions have been tested. Most athletes want and very much deserve the physical and mental break from a training routine.

The fatigue can often be as much psychological as physical. J.J. Clark, a track and cross-country coach at the University of Tennessee, talked about the transition his elite athletes go through: "The training is very stressful. They need a mental break. They don't want to have to worry about what time they get up or what they eat. A lot of them, after long careers, just say, 'That's it.'"

After having strict structure around a routine and workout schedule, it's nice to have that break. This is a break to heal old injuries and pay attention to the areas of an athlete's life neglected during competition training. But after the break, when there are no more coaches, it can be difficult to find motivation to pick up any exercise again.

When I first left rowing, I loved not having to work out. I was always a naturally active person, so I thought when the time was right I would pick up right where I left off, working out most days of the week. However, a few weeks turned into a few months, and before I knew it, I became the person googling "how to get in shape." I joined the closest gym to my new apartment, went the first day, and that was it. I tried convincing myself to go, but I just couldn't. There was no attendance. No added punishment for being late. No teammates to push me through. No trainer to instruct what to do. The gym was somewhere I used to feel comfortable, but now it was a mix of overwhelm and sadness for missing something I wouldn't be able to find again.

Not only was I not motivated, but I started looking down on myself for not going to the gym.

Not only was I not motivated, but I started looking down on myself for not going to the gym. So much of my worth was in the image I had of myself being an athlete, in shape, working out, and always caring about my health. I felt less valuable now. I was no longer the same image I had of myself. Can you really call yourself an athlete if you haven't been to the gym in three months?

REST IS IMPORTANT:

Even though I was fighting this battle internally and felt alone, it's something most athletes face when leaving sports. Former NCAA volleyball champion Victoria Garrick found that when she retired she no longer had the motivation to train. She described her transition in a YouTube video: "I was always working out, I had a coach, I had a team, I was pushing my body to its limits. And now I don't have to do that. So, I didn't want to do that."

Victoria had been an athlete her entire life and spent years pushing her body to its limit. She knew how to train well, she won NCAA volleyball championships after all, but now that it wasn't a part of her job, she didn't want to do any of it anymore. The things that motivate an athlete to train— the medals, records, adrenaline, and competition—aren't there in the real world. When an athlete trains at the top standard they have set for themselves, anything less feels like just that: less.

When Victoria was done competing, she saw some of her non-athlete friends going to group fitness classes like Soul Cycle and CorePower Yoga. She says, "I just thought I trained so much more intensely. None of this was even worth doing. . . . There was no way to simulate the workouts of my standard because I didn't have an Olympic lifting set and have a gym and all the resources available for me anymore."

> When an athlete trains at the top standard they have set for themselves, anything less feels like just that: less.

She admits that at the time, she thought she was too good for standard group fitness workouts. She was holding herself to the same standard she had while competing for a national title. The combination of no motivation to continue the same training, along with a lack of resources, led her to take a break from working out completely. However, the rest was needed, and she was eventually able to pick up working out again.

Victoria found a healthy balance between rest and exercise after taking a few months completely without exercise. She slowly started incorporating movement again by trying dance classes and yoga. "It's fun to try different things because now you can move your body in a way that makes you happy," she said.

Luckily, Victoria was able to find another form of exercise that she was excited to do again. The issue with this period of rest is that it can be hard to recognize when to transition out of it. Although rest is necessary, as in the beginning of any off-season, this one is different. The off-season never stops. Retired athletes never turn into "in-season" athletes again. An athlete needs rest, but they also need a healthy relationship with exercise. This will help prevent them from burnout or, on the other side of the spectrum, inactivity. I think we all know a story of a former athlete who used to be in the best shape of their life, only to never touch gym equipment again.

TOO MUCH REST:

The reason we all know a story like this is because it is very common. Research shows that there's no significant difference in exercise patterns between former athletes and non-athletes. Both are equally likely to become couch potatoes. Whether someone was a star athlete breaking records or never made it out of little league baseball, their past doesn't dictate their future workout routine.

This isn't necessarily a bad thing. After prioritizing sports for so long it might be time for a change. Especially if transitioning to another phase of life, an athlete might need to put their focus somewhere else. But athletes should be aware of this finding. Just because they were a star athlete and disciplined to wake up at 6 a.m. on Saturdays for four years doesn't mean this will translate into life afterward.

When speaking to Julianne O'Connell, one of my friends who is a former three-sport athlete, she said she also struggled to pick up a workout routine after retirement. While in school, she played a different sport with each season and was a varsity basketball, soccer, and lacrosse player. Her typical off-season training was to play the next season's sport. This is not what many would consider a time of rest. Julianne did this all four years and, after she graduated high school, she quit competitive sports.

Like many athletes, Julianne took a complete break from sports. This gave her time to focus on adjusting to a new school, making friends outside of athletics, and learning what life was like without sports. After a few months, she decided to try working out again.

Julianne recalled, "I tried to do intramurals, but it wasn't the same. I had played competitive sports throughout my entire life, and these people were like, 'Let's have fun.' I don't know how to do that. I don't know how to play sports for fun; I played to compete." This is a mindset in which a lot of athletes get stuck. As we saw in Victoria's case, she was used to training intensely and couldn't break that barrier for a while. Julianne struggled with how to play her sport as a pickup game just for fun.

> I don't know how to play sports for fun; I played to compete.

Since the friendly pickup games weren't suiting her, Julianne tried to find a more competitive way to keep playing basketball. She said, "I started a club basketball team in college, and I made it as competitive as I could. I also realized that we had other things going on; we had friends, we had school, and we had work commitments." Julianne recognized her life was no longer centered around sports. Instead of dropping everything to travel for a game, she now had other priorities she had to balance out. This left her in the same spot that it leaves most former athletes, no more active than their non-sporty counterparts.

Expert Dr. Erin Reifsteck has a background in both living and studying this subject. She was a field hockey goalkeeper in college and is now an assistant professor in the Department of Kinesiology at the University of North Carolina at Greensboro. "There is an assumption that athletes know how to be active, have always been active, and therefore will always be active, but the evidence suggests that is not necessarily the case," said Dr. Reifsteck in the *UNCG Research Magazine*. "Priorities change, [and] former athletes turn their focus towards finding a job, starting a family or pursuing new opportunities."

Since athletes don't have balance while competing, it can be difficult to figure out when they have freedom of choice. They're used to dropping everything to dedicate time, money, and more to their goals. When new priorities come in the way, one of the things they might drop is working out.

At this point in adapting to life after sport, the benefits of exercise should not be ignored. Since former athletes are in a vulnerable place to feel heightened depression and anxiety from the transition, exercise might be a helpful addition to their routine. Daniel Gould wrote in his textbook, "Many researchers, clinicians, and laypeople have observed that physical activity enhances feelings of well-being, in particular by reducing anxiety and depression. In addition, in the last five to ten years, reviews of the literature have concluded that exercise is related to decreases in anxiety and depression as well as increases in feelings of general well-being."

Exercise is something that athletes are used to using as their outlet to let out these emotions. It's their stress relief, and it brings structure and routine. Not only are they experiencing triggers for anxiety and depression, but now they might be removing the activity that originally helped decrease those emotions. It's important to create a healthy relationship with rest as soon as possible in this transition to create a healthy routine that enhances a former athlete's new life.

STEP ONE. S - SLOW DOWN:

As athletes, the "S" we're used to is "sacrifice." The "S" we need to learn is "slow down." To find a healthy balance between rest and exercise, you need to slow down. If you continue at the rate you were going before, it will likely lead to burnout or even injury. On the other hand, if you become inactive in your new off-season lifestyle, it can become unhealthy on the other end of the spectrum. By slowing down, you can be more intentional in incorporating rest into your routine in an appropriate amount.

> By slowing down you can be more intentional in incorporating rest into your routine in an appropriate amount.

Rest is a necessary part of the process. Rejuvenation requires rest. Rest is enjoyable, not something to stress about. It takes time to be able to see how staying active can fit into your new lifestyle, or sometimes even what your new lifestyle will be. So don't force yourself into a routine just because it's what you think needs to happen. In this new period of life, athletics and working out must come with much more balance than before.

Chances are, as an athlete, you already have some ideas in your head of what rest means. Sometimes athletes can feel guilty for resting because it's not something they've had the ability to do consistently. Some athletes view it as a waste of time and others view it as a reward for all their hard work. No matter your thoughts on rest as an athlete, you need to have a good relationship with adding it now to feel good about having a balanced routine. Balance prevents burnout. If you're unsure how to look at rest, consider this a helpful reminder:

Exercise and rest are needed for different reasons. Exercise is known to improve your health, self-esteem, and support healthy sleep, in addition to many other benefits. Rest aids in muscle recovery, reduces the risk of injury, and prevents fatigue. Both are equally important and will complement each other in giving you enough energy and strength to show up confidently in your daily activities. There's no right or wrong amount of rest to give your body. Just be aware of how you're feeling, and you'll be able to tell when you've been favoring one too much over the other.

There are multiple steps for developing a healthy balance in your life after your period of rest. Now that you know the importance of slowing down and adding rest, you can build from here. The first place to start is something often overlooked since athletes can be used to eating anything they want: nutrition.

＊ ＊ ＊

To hear more tips on how to relax, rest, recover, and enjoy the off-season, listen to my podcast episode "Life Changes and Big Transition? First Step to Start the Journey Strong" at http://emilycoffman.org/life-transitions/

CHAPTER 2:

FUELING YOUR LIFESTYLE

———

"We have to be smaller, skinnier, and lighter—and stronger at the same time. There's a lot of discipline involved."

—JOHN VELAZQUEZ, FOUR-TIME KENTUCKY DERBY JOCKEY WINNER

Competing as a coxswain comes down to one thing . . . being 110 pounds. Coxswains get weighed before every competition, and if you are underweight, you have to carry sandbags to make up the difference. This is dead weight and weighs down the boat. If you are over 110 pounds, then you had extra weight and weigh down the boat.

This put me in a very narrow window of sixteen ounces. I spent seven years trying to gain weight and then lose weight so I could stay at the perfect number. I was in this same position from my sophomore year of high school to my senior year of college. Through my first period, freshman fifteen stage, and all-around maturing as an adult, I had to maintain the same 110 pounds.

Since I was already living an active lifestyle and constantly at the gym, it was easiest to try to change the scale through my eating habits. When I started the sport, I was around ninety-five pounds and would force myself to overeat before competitions. I would go to Chipotle and get the largest burrito possible and try to eat it all right before weigh-ins. This left me feeling uncomfortable, bloated, and nauseous all at the same time. Then two years later, when the burrito eating had caught up to me, the scale jumped up to 120 pounds. I would then prepare for competition by eating and drinking as little as possible. I would be hungry and dehydrated trying to get the scale to read 110 pounds at just the right moment.

Was this healthy? No. But it's what was needed given the circumstances. I spent a lot of time as an athlete thinking about what I was going to eat. My eating had to satisfy the scale, optimize my practice performance, and be timed around travel, weigh-ins, and spending multiple hours on the water. My eating was rarely dictated by what I wanted most, but what would suit my body best for rowing.

> My eating was rarely dictated by what I wanted most, but what would suit my body best for rowing.

After sports come to an end, a lot changes. But an athlete's eating habits tend to stay the same. It's not like an athlete wakes up the day after competition and their taste buds have changed. With so much change happening, it's nice to have something stay the same, and eating habits can feel like a comfort. Once an athlete no longer has to prepare their body for anything, they might not think what they were eating has to change. So, does it?

EATING LIKE AN ATHLETE:

In a podcast interview, former athlete Kelsey Anselmi discussed her eating habits after competition ended. Kelsey grew up playing every sport and always watched them on TV with her dad. After years of trying multiple sports, her parents made her choose one on which she would focus, and she chose basketball. She was a great athlete and got recruited to Benedictine College where she played all four years.

While in college, she didn't pay too much attention to what she was eating. "I was in my best fitness, working out three hours a day, lifting weights, but I was still eating fast food, which was absolutely disgusting, but it was my choice." She knew that her eating wasn't the healthiest, but since she was working out every single day and staying on top of her fitness, she didn't notice any effect to her body.

After college, she stuck with the same diet and started seeing some changes to her weight. She recalls, "No one ever told me about food. I was in the best shape of my life eating pure crap. My metabolism was great, thank God, because I stayed at a decent weight during college, but when I left college, my metabolism caught up to me."

A big misconception is that athletes know a lot about nutrition given how in shape they are during competition. The reality is their physique is due in large part to their rigorous training schedule, not a solid

> No one ever told me about food. I was in the best shape of my life eating pure crap.

nutrition plan. In a recent research study called "Athletes: Fit but Unhealthy?", Philip Maffetone and Paul Laursen found that although athletes are very fit, many are not healthy. They describe the difference as, "fitness and health can be defined separately: fitness describes the ability to perform a given exercise task, and health explains a person's state of well-being, where physiological systems work in harmony."

They found that athletes who fit the description of being fit but unhealthy can be given the term "overtraining syndrome." Athletes may think that they're healthy because they're in shape, but the truth is many athletes are training too much and not eating to fuel their body properly. Philip said, "We propose that two primary drivers may contribute to the development of the overtraining syndrome, namely high training intensity and the modern-day, highly processed, high glycemic diet." The glycemic index measures how quickly foods raise a person's blood sugar, and a high glycemic diet can cause harmful blood sugar spikes.

Even though nutrition is a big factor in performance, athletes tend to have the mindset of "I can eat this and not gain any weight." This may be true but doesn't set the athlete up for good habits after sport. Athletes, in general, eat highly processed diets while competing, and they will continue their current eating plan after sport because they have never known another diet.

Kelsey fell back on the eating habits she already had when her routine started to change. She said, "I was still on a fast-food diet, and I was not taking care of myself. I was a brand-new teacher, I was coaching varsity athletics, and I was saying yes to everything." She thought she had no other choice but to continue eating fast-food. She was a recent graduate trying to balance her new job and added responsibilities. Everything else in her life was overwhelming, so she didn't want to throw in the complication of learning nutrition. She finally hit a turning point when she stopped coaching and was fully out of the athletic world.

"Once I stopped coaching, I really was taken aback at my figure because I had gained weight. I was up almost fifteen pounds. I wasn't working out," she recalled, "I was just so upset with myself because I am an athlete. I used to do the hardest workouts in my life, and now suddenly I can't even get my foot up off the couch."

A lot of athletes have seen a situation like this happen to them. "At first, the body can handle that huge energy surplus, because it's still expecting to exercise," said Jeff Kotterman, a board member of the National Association of Sports Nutrition, "But after a while, even for the most gifted athletes, that extra dessert or fatty food is no longer dealt with the same way."

Kelsey was frustrated because she became so different than the person she used to be. She was no longer the athlete that she spent most of her life identifying as. The first twenty-five years of her life were dedicated to sport, and now her body was no longer recognizable.

"What happens to the athlete is not that different than what happens to a lot of people that come on Jenny Craig," said director of nutrition at Jenny Craig, Lisa Talamini, one of the world's largest weight management companies. "Maybe a few years ago they were more active, burning more calories daily. Now they're sitting in front of their computers at work

. . . [for an athlete], it just happens over a faster time period with a larger number of calories."

This is normal for an athlete to experience. They go from working out as a full-time job to having to fit it into a new routine. Their calorie burn quickly drops, but their eating habits do not. That is something that usually takes longer for them to change.

After gaining the fifteen pounds, Kelsey decided that was it. She was going to become the athlete that she once was. She realized the difference this time was going to be how she fueled her body. She recalled, "I was like, 'Screw this, you're going to get your butt back in shape. There's no more excuses, there's no more BS, get off the couch and go. Use your body. You are twenty-eight years old. Stop making excuses. There are fifty-five-year-olds completing Ironmans, and you can't even run a mile, and you're a former college athlete.'"

When she retired from being an athlete, she never stopped eating like she was working out as one. She knew that she had to adjust her nutrition plan and decided this time she would focus on eating to fuel her for an upcoming triathlon.

Many athletes who don't pay special attention to their nutrition while competing continue with their same eating habits. These eating habits seem to be a non-issue when competing because an athlete is fit but unhealthy.

The answer to this might sound easy. Shouldn't former athletes just learn nutrition after so they can start eating healthier? Yes, but nutrition is a huge topic to cover, and just like anything else, it can't and won't be learned overnight. There's something a former athlete should learn first about their eating habits before taking on nutrition: their hunger cues.

LISTENING TO YOUR BODY:

Bri Collete, a volleyball player from Canada, had this issue when she finished competing. After retiring, she found it difficult to pick up on her hunger cues because she was used to the consistent schedule of always working out which led to always being hungry.

She said in a recent podcast, "It's hard going from a place of being hungry all the time and eating whatever you want to now not knowing what your internal cues are, not knowing what's full and hungry and how that shifts every day. You were just used to being hungry all the time. So how do you get to know your body?"

She used to be in a constant state of burning a lot of calories and always needing to replenish them. After retirement, she was faced with things like rest days and vacations where her body's needs were changing. When she had these breaks for the first time, she faced the challenge of *"When am I hungry? When am I full? I'm just used to eating, eating, eating."*

Later, she became a volleyball coach for her old team. She was still in athletics, and although she was able to help them with drills, she

> You were just used to being hungry all the time. So how do you get to know your body?

was nowhere as active as she used to be. Now that she wasn't training for volleyball, she had the freedom to exercise however she wanted and eat however she wanted. "Food became different because I didn't have to eat a certain way before or after practice or fuel my body in a certain way. I felt this freedom. All of a sudden, all these foods were available to me. I didn't have to hold back on eating them, and so the freedom and all of this time on my own was this perfect equation for developing some unhealthy eating habits and obsessions with food and exercise combined."

> It was kind of this perfect equation for developing some unhealthy eating habits.

The new freedom combined with unhealthy eating habits quickly led to an obsession with over-exercise and food. In Bri's head, if she kept exercising like she used to, then she could keep eating however she'd like. She wanted to have the same mentality and the same lifestyle that she had as an athlete, so she kept pushing herself to those extremes. She finally came to a tipping point when she realized she was no longer able to keep this up long-term.

Bri recalled, "I got scared into trying to listen to my body because I said, 'Man, I can't keep this up. I can't keep pushing myself past these limits of feeling like I'm this twenty-one-year-old volleyball player, competitive athlete. I can't keep that up forever, and I can't keep exercising in order to control my food intake.'"

She was never taught another way of doing things, so she kept doing the same routine she had as an athlete. She didn't have an end goal of what she was working towards, she was just stuck on this hamster wheel of exercise and food, which turned into a vicious cycle. She learned that this was no longer sustainable, and she knew the issue started back at her eating habits.

She just wanted to learn how to eat normally, without obsession. She didn't want to worry about if she was eating too much and, if she did, didn't want to feel like she had to work out to make up for it. She didn't want to feel out of control of her body and her eating.

I spoke with Katie Spada, a former US National Team member for synchronized swimming who now specializes in fueling former athletes. She's a registered dietitian. I asked her about the first steps an athlete should take in adjusting their nutrition after competition. Katie said, "One of the biggest things is hunger fullness. When you're an athlete, oftentimes you have to put hunger fullness to the side to implement practical hunger. Maybe you're not hungry after practice, but you know you need to eat anyways."

Hunger and fullness cues might sound like a basic concept; you eat when you're hungry and stop when you're full. So, why do former athletes need to pay attention to this?

While in competition, these cues often have to be ignored. Athletes know they need to eat something before a competition, regardless of how they might be feeling. Rowing competitions were always a full-day event. I remember leaving our hotel room before sunrise not expecting to have a meal again until after the race, hours later. It wasn't an option to not eat at breakfast. I wouldn't have the option to eat again for hours. All athletes know this. Even if they don't wake up hungry, they have a schedule of when to eat.

Also, different sports have expectations on how your body needs to perform that often isn't naturally occurring. Katie described, "Maybe you had to ignore your hunger because you needed to lose weight for your sport. Maybe you need to ignore your fullness because you need to gain muscle, you need to gain weight for your sport. Whatever place you're coming from, toning back into hunger and fullness is the first step, and oftentimes we don't even know what the signs of hunger are."

An athlete only needs to remember an important concept they've used before: intuition for their body.

Though many athletes struggle with nutrition after their professional careers are over, an athlete only needs to remember an important concept they've used before: intuition for their body. Athletes already have practice being in tune with their bodies. They must know what type of pain they can push through and what type leads to injury. They need to know when to give it their all and when to pace themselves for later in the game. Athletes are good at listening to their bodies' physical needs, and the same intuition can be applied to hunger and fullness. Knowing the needs of the body is something in which athletes have experience, and practicing intuitive eating can help them get their nutrition back on track.

Katie explained, "I always say athletes are the most equipped for intuitive eating and mindful eating because we do have such a great understanding of our bodies. We've had to be so intuitive to get them to succeed and be able to perform, when other people who haven't reached this level, they have to learn that from the beginning. So as athletes, we start at an advantage in multiple things in life but in our nutrition as well."

STEP TWO. I - INTUITIVELY EAT:

Listening to your hunger cues is included in one of the ten principles of intuitive eating. Intuitive eating is an approach to eating that places your body's needs and signals as priority over following a particular meal plan. It was founded by Evelyn Tribole and Elyse Resch, and many people read their book *Intuitive Eating: a Revolutionary Anti-Diet Approach* to be educated on their perspective and techniques.

The second principle "Honor Your Hunger" says, "Keep your body biologically fed with adequate energy and carbohydrates. Otherwise, you can trigger a primal drive to overeat. Once you reach the moment of excessive hunger, all intentions of moderate, conscious eating are fleeting and irrelevant."

One of the issues with former athletes' nutrition after sports is that they continue to overeat to the level of food they were consuming when active every day. Now that they are less active, they also require less food. The easiest way to avoid overeating is to notice your hunger cues and not let yourself get too hungry.

Evelyn rates hunger and fullness sensations on a scale from zero to ten. Zero is described as "painfully hungry. This is primal hunger, which is very intense and urgent," and goes up to ten: "Painfully full, stuffed. May feel nauseated." Many dietitians recommend staying between a three and a seven on the scale which would mean you stay between "hungry and ready to eat, but there is no urgency. It's a polite hunger," and "comfortable fullness, which feels satisfied and content."

This means being able to notice when your body is starting to get hungry and eating then instead of waiting until you physically can't go any longer without eating. This could look like making sure you eat breakfast in the morning, so you don't have to wait until lunch, or packing snacks so you can hold yourself over until big meals.

While this might take some practice to get used to, the authors offer some general advice to follow: "Take care not to get overly hungry or ravenous. If this is difficult for you to gauge, a general guideline is to go no longer than five waking hours without eating."

Intuitive eating is something that takes time to learn but puts you back in control of your body and your decisions. It's not an overnight process, but Kelsey found that making the decision to focus on her health and nutrition brought her back to the ambitious athlete she used to be. Kelsey described her journey, "It's been slow but I'm thankful that it finally happened because it reconnected me with those principles of being an athlete. Being disciplined to get up to go for a run, to complete the mission, and to set the goals. So, while it was fun while it lasted—the whole value meal thing and fast-food thing—I'm so thankful for this last six months of just being recommitted to myself."

> Ending sports without changing your eating habits is like showing up to your job with your college textbook.

Ending sports without changing your eating habits is like showing up to your job with your college textbook. Intuitive eating is one of the first things an athlete can do to slowly adjust to life after sport. At this point in the journey, an athlete has gone through mental stress, has decreased their level of working out, and has likely continued eating the same way. This could lead to physical body changes like increased weight and decreased muscle. The final part of the new unknown is how to deal with these body changes.

* * *

To hear more from Katie Spada on Intuitive Eating and former athlete nutrition, listen to our conversation at emilycoffman. org/fuelingformerathletes

CHAPTER 3:

EMBRACING THE CHANGES

"The pursuit of this muscular ideal takes over people's lives. They become obsessed with it. They can't function in their daily life outside of pursuing this ideal and it can lead to depression, missing school or work, and losing their ability to do basic living tasks."

—*DR. JASON NAGATA, RESEARCHER*

This never-ending off-season can feel like a vacation at first. No one telling you what to do, unlimited rest days, and the ability to eat whatever, whenever you want. This sounds like a dream, doesn't it? But you know how the saying goes: "Too much of a good thing can be bad." The "bad" that happens to most athletes is seen in their bodies through muscle loss or weight gain. This is a normal occurrence after working out less, but it's a foreign concept to many athletes who have spent years in top shape.

By nature of my position, I was used to the process of weight gain and weight loss. But even if I was used to the changes physically, this doesn't mean that I was mentally prepared. One hundred and ten pounds was such an important number to me that it became a criterion for my success. If I only weighed myself one time per week for the seven and a half years I competed, I still would have weighed myself four hundred times. I weighed myself far more than just once per week.

After I retired from rowing, I no longer had a need to weigh myself, but I could feel myself gaining weight. I knew that it this was due to my lack of exercise, but was it okay to gain weight? How much weight gain was normal? What weight should my body be? I spent so many years focused on one specific number that I wasn't even sure what my body should look like when not striving for the scale to say 110.0.

> Was it okay to gain weight? How much weight gain is normal?

I developed an unhealthy relationship with how I viewed my body. Even though 110 pounds was an arbitrary number for a sport I was no longer playing, it still felt like that was part of me. I almost thought if I could stay that weight then I would still be seen as an athlete, but if I gained the weight then it would be time for me to acknowledge the end of my career. Instead of fighting this change, I wish I had taken a different approach.

WEIGHT CHANGES:

I talked to one of my old college teammates, Chloé Campbell, about her transition leaving sports and how it led to her pursuit of weight loss. Before she was a coxswain on the rowing team with me, she trained to be a collegiate rower. Chloé looked forward to being a rower at the University of Alabama, but during her senior year of high school had an unsuccessful elbow surgery that made her unable to row. This was hard for her to accept, since her strength was a huge part of her identity. Growing up, her dad was a bodybuilder and she had trained next to him since she was little.

When I sat down with Chloé she recalled, "I put a lot of my identity into my size and how much I could lift. I was a really cool kid at school who was stronger than half the men were. Like, 'you didn't want to mess with her because she could legit beat you up' type of situation." Strength was an important thing to Chloé because she is also small. At just five feet tall, she took pride in the fact that she was one of the strongest girls she knew.

But after her surgery she only had 50 percent of her strength in her arm, and she no longer kept the same strong appearance. Chloé felt discouraged watching her body shrink. She tried working out by doing cardio or leg-only exercises, but she could tell that she was losing her muscles.

At the same time, she also had a bad reaction to her pain medication from the surgery. The medicine made her lose her appetite, so she wasn't eating enough and was losing weight fast. This turned into a very dangerous cycle. "I don't have to claim I'm starving myself, but at the end of the day, taking something to keep me from being hungry is starving yourself. But I thought I could just blame it on the pills. It was fine because I had a prescription for them."

Months after needing the pills for recovery from surgery, she was still taking them. Now that Chloé was no longer an athlete and

> We grew up in a time where girls weren't supposed to be muscular, they were supposed to be little twigs.

"the strong one," she had a mind shift and decided she would be the skinny one. People around her fed into this idea too. She said, "We grew up in a time where girls weren't supposed to be muscular, they were supposed to be little twigs—but I was never that type of person. I wanted to be muscular. But when it went from people accusing my muscle for fat to hearing, 'Oh my gosh, you're so beautiful' after I lost the weight . . . that was fuel to the fire for not eating."

It took getting to an unhealthy level of restriction for Chloé to realize that she had to make a change. She was no longer a competing athlete and had to accept that she wouldn't have the same athletic body she had years earlier. She says, "To accept who I am as a non-athlete, I have to be willing to accept that I'm probably going to have a little bit more fat in places that I don't naturally exercise." Chloé's story isn't strictly about weight loss. It's about athletes trying to physically fit into a non-athletic world. Chloé wasn't trying to lose weight because she was unhealthy; she was trying to be skinny to be satisfied with her body again.

Olympic Alpine Skier Lindsey Vonn has also been open to trying to fit into the non-athletic world. After winning an Olympic gold medal she became an American celebrity, invited to red carpet events and Hollywood parties. In her book *Strong is the New Beautiful* she said, "Before the Olympics, I had been immersed in my own aesthetic world, the world of skiing, where everyone looks like I do. . . . But now I was in a realm where being skinny seemed to matter more than being healthy, and certainly more than being fit. I started to question myself."

An athlete surrounded by teammates who look like them tends to think about their body less. Teammates care about the body's performance, not whether it looks good or not. But when an athlete is no longer in sports, how do they fit into the rest of the world?

Lindsey wasn't retired at this point but was out of her normal athletics bubble. After being in the limelight because of her skiing accomplishments, she went back to training with that experience still weighing on her. She said, "These insecurities haunted me into the following season, and I became more concerned with how I looked in the mirror than with how strong I felt in the gym or on the hill."

Lindsey Vonn. One of the best alpine skiers in the world. Record-breaking four-time World Cup overall champion. Her strength

> I became more concerned with how I looked in the mirror than with how strong I felt in the gym.

and muscles were celebrated by so many people. Yet, she became insecure and questioned how her body was perceived by the outside world. Her shift in focus started to affect her performance. She questioned, "I knew that I was hurting my career, and for what? My perception of someone else's perception of what was beautiful?"

It's a sad fact, but many athletes have concerns about their bodies' appearance. Especially when they don't fit society's ideals, athletes go into retirement feeling insecure and think they should change to fit in. This type of mindset can trigger unhealthy habits, even if the athlete has never experienced any before.

If an athlete is unhappy in their body, this doesn't just affect weight loss and weight gain efforts, but it can affect all areas of their life.

"A person's evaluation of their body contributes to their overall self-concept. A person's self-perception dictates thoughts, beliefs, behaviors, and feelings. Thus, negative body image can be especially pervasive, both directly and indirectly influencing many aspects of a person's life," states the *Journal of Kinesiology & Wellness*. "Even seemingly unrelated life domains, such as the ability to confidently carry out everyday tasks and the ability to create and maintain relationships, are impacted by body image experiences."

We know that athletes in retirement are already facing a lot of psychological change, and their body image is another influence on their mental state during this transition. Both Chloé and Lindsey got out of their unhealthy patterns by focusing back on what kept them happy and healthy. Changing their body wasn't making them any healthier or any happier, it was only bringing down their self-confidence.

After Lindsey missed the overall World Champion title by just three points the following year, she resolved that she would fully commit to training her hardest. She knew that winning the title and performing her best meant so much more for her than fitting into the non-athlete world.

BODY IMAGE:

Even if body image issues and weight are mostly talked about through a female lens, it affects male athletes just as often. In an article posted by Team USA, Dr. Melissa Streno, a clinical psychologist who specializes in athletic performance and its intersection with disordered eating and body image issues, talked about how body image issues appear in men. "People hear eating disorder, and they automatically assume that it's a female issue," said Streno. "But there are issues like muscle dysmorphia, which is when someone is trying to achieve a specific body type or a certain amount of muscle to look a particular way. We see a lot of that with males. Now we're seeing a lot more men who need treatment and seek out support."

No one is immune to body image issues. Body dissatisfaction and weight loss and gain aren't exclusive to the athletic community. It impacts almost all communities at any age. However, something that largely affects athletes in this situation over others is the presence of body dysmorphic disorder.

Body dysmorphic disorder, also known as body dysmorphia, is defined as "a body-image disorder characterized by persistent and intrusive preoccupations with an imagined or slight defect in one's appearance." When an athlete's body starts changing after competition it's common for them to notice slight differences. Even though no one else might notice a less than five percent change in muscle mass, if that change affects how an athlete performs at the gym, then they will likely quickly notice it. After years of pushing their body and constantly improving performance, when the body starts getting weaker (even slightly) it can cause a domino effect of negative thoughts and habits.

Athletes can spend a lot of time thinking about their bodies. It's the vehicle that allows them to perform how they do. Athletes put a lot of value in their bodies, but one of the athletes I spoke to ran into the question of "What happens when you stop competing and your body is no longer valued?"

Elena Sturdivant was one of my teammates in college, and after she retired from rowing she had a lot of other responsibilities on which to focus. She started law school a few months after retiring, got a new job, and had to plan for her upcoming wedding. Now that she was no longer a full-time athlete, exercise was not her top priority. Right out of competition, she didn't pick up any sort of workout routine. "I call my first year out of rowing my year to pasture. People that know animals know you retire them to pasture when they're past their working years. My fitness routine was nothing in any way, shape, or form for at least six months."

She viewed her physical performance as past its prime. Because of this, she stopped her workout routine completely. A few months into retirement she was getting ready for her swearing ceremony (the equivalence of a white coat ceremony for doctors) to start law school. She went to buy a suit and found that nothing fit.

She was used to clothing being hard to find. She has always been tall with long arms and wide shoulders, but this time was different. She was in the middle of a plus-sized store, and nothing fit. Even in the plus-sized options, she couldn't find anything that buttoned and looked flattering. She recalls, "That was a really hard morning to wake up and hate what I saw in the mirror and know that I had made all the decisions that led me there. I felt like that was liberation, and now I was stuck in this kind of prison that I'd built for myself."

This was a hard realization to come to because less than a year earlier she was a successful Division I Athlete. However, Elena's body image issues didn't start when she transitioned out of sports. This was something that she struggled with while still an athlete. At the time, she didn't acknowledge her feelings. Looking back, she started to process where the thoughts came from and realized that when she was an athlete, she had the mindset of, "As long as I'm fast enough, what I look like doesn't matter. As long as I'm fast enough, what I weigh doesn't matter. As long as I'm fast enough, how I feel about myself doesn't matter." She told me, "That was really hard to come to peace with as well, because once you're not justifying what you feel about yourself with something positive, you're just left with what you have."

Her body image wasn't as big of a deal while she was competing because her body was valued. It's what allowed her to be fast and be the athlete that she

> Once you're not justifying what you feel about yourself with something positive, you're just left with what you have.

was. But now that her weight and body weren't linked with anything positive, she was left feeling trapped by it. This is something that is common among athletes. A study on *Retired Athletes and the Intersection of Food and Body* stated: "Nutrition and body composition are functions of an athlete's occupation, sometimes creating a complex relationship with food and body for the individual. Athletic retirement is a disruption to this already complex relationship that provides an environment to precipitate compensatory behaviors."

Elena had to disconnect her identity and her worth from her body image. She says, "I was embarrassed to tell people that I had been an athlete because I thought, 'They're going to think that rowing was a joke,' because I looked like a cow. And there's no way that somebody who's actually good at rowing would look like that." Elena had previously had an issue with body confidence and the extra weight didn't help. She started slowly working out and began a weight loss program that got her back to her original goals. She was proud of herself, not just for losing the weight but mostly because she got back into eating habits and a schedule that worked well for her and made her happy.

Over two years later, Elena is now married and graduated from law school. She has a steady workout routine that isn't fueled by weight loss but by maintenance. She stopped putting so much worth into her body and started exercising for the pure joy of it. She still ergs [exercise on the indoor rowing machine] like she did while she was a rower, but with a very different focus. She describes, "It's such a mentally happy place for me. I don't even think it has that much to do with exercise. It has more to do with focusing, and it's very calming for me."

STEP THREE. D – DEVELOP BODY ACCEPTANCE:

To change your view of your body, it's important to move to a place of body acceptance. Body acceptance means that you accept your body regardless of not being completely satisfied with all aspects of it. You don't have to view your body as perfect to take care of it, and you don't need to be constantly trying to change it. You can just let your body be. As is.

Researcher Caroline Laure wrote a research paper on this topic called *Examining Body Image in Retired Collegiate Volleyball Players.* She said, "Bodily changes, including changes in weight, muscle mass, and physical competencies may occur as a result of the discontinuation of regular, intense training. If the former athlete perceives these physical changes negatively, their physical self-concept, body image, and overall self-esteem may be adversely affected."

Body acceptance is less about what is physically happening to the body and more about how it is perceived. The first step in body acceptance is to know that change is normal. Your body will change after sport, just like it probably did during sport.

If you go into retirement already acknowledging that your routine is changing and your body composition will likely change with it, then you'll be less likely to react negatively.

Comfort - Approval = Acceptance

Comfort is knowing that what your body is experiencing is normal and not something that has to be fought against. Approval comes from our need of validation and wrongly putting our worth in our bodies' appearance. Comfort minus the need for approval equals acceptance. To reach body acceptance, athletes need to drop the worth we put on our bodies that has been engrained in us for so long. Your body doesn't need to prove itself through approval from coaches, parents, teammates, or through more accomplishments. Your body leads you to your accomplishments. Your body is not your accomplishment.

In my case, I found acceptance after tossing the scale out completely. If I didn't have to be at a certain number anymore, then why should I care about what the number is at all? The scale allowed me to put pressure on myself that there was a "right" or "wrong" number to be. After a short period of gaining weight my body, appetite, and exercise routine adapted to my new schedule, and I was able to add in healthy eating and workouts without trying to change my body's appearance.

By taking comfort in allowing change to happen and separating your body from your worth, you're able to reach a place of body acceptance.

Now that you've experienced your new routine and seen the changes that come with it, it's time to address how to move on from sports. In the beginning, everything is still unknown.

You might feel uncomfortable with some of the physical and emotional changes, but you have the enjoyment of it being off-season and being able to work out and eat how you'd like. Once you start to notice long-term changes (like in your figure), it can bring up more feelings of confusion and insecurity. This turns into what I like to call the "messy middle" of transitioning out of sports. First step: how to move on from clinging to an athletic identity.

* * *

Listen to my podcast episode "Develop a Relationship of Trust with Yourself and Not the Scale" for more tips on body acceptance and removing your worth from your body at http://emilycoffman.org/ditch-the-scale/

PHASE TWO: THE MESSY MIDDLE

CHAPTER 4:

THE INNER ATHLETE

"Your sport does not define you, but it has helped to define how you will handle future situations. It has taught you discipline, commitment, time management, and teamwork, and it has shown you the joy of success and the heartbreak of defeat."

—*LAUREN LINK, RD, CSSD*

Have you ever felt like sports were your purpose and direction in life?

As athletes, most of us have been training since we were children. We have always been on a team, training at any sort of level, and it occupied most areas of our life. I remember while still competing, whenever I talked to anyone outside of my team, the conversation always circled back to what I was accomplishing in rowing. Relatives would ask me, "How is the season going?" Friends would ask me, "When's your next race?" I felt like the most exciting thing about me was that I was an athlete.

It wasn't just how others viewed me. It was also how I viewed myself. In college, I would introduce myself as, "I'm Emily and I'm on the rowing team." I would show up anywhere with an automatic group of friends because I had my teammates around. I would walk around campus in my sports gear and anyone who even looked at me could automatically identify me as an athlete, and this was something that I loved.

It was a great part of being an athlete, and it was a way that I felt automatically accepted. But there came a point after competition where identifying myself as an athlete went from something I was proud of to something that became upsetting. I realized the more I identified myself as an athlete when I was no longer competing, the more I felt like I was living in the past. It's really cliché, but it felt like going back to my glory days. I didn't want to be that high school hero who keeps bringing up their past. I did it, though, because that was an identity that I had loved.

> The more I identified myself as an athlete when I was no longer competing, the more I felt like I was living in the past.

Moving on from athletics is something that's tough for former athletes going through this transition. It's their hobby, entertainment, community, and a part of their identity. Maybe they aren't ready for their identity to go away. Maybe they don't want it to go away because it's the only one they've ever known, and a lot of athletes wear their status with pride. Before we talk about creating a new identity, let's talk about letting go of the old one.

AN ATHLETE'S IDENTITY:

Someone who is very familiar with the importance of identity is retired football quarterback Max Browne. As a top football recruit during high school, Max Browne could go to any college program he wanted and get recruited to any football team. While still in high school, he was named the 2012 Gatorade National Football Player of the Year, USA Today All USA Offensive Player of the Year, Prep Star All American Dream Team, and ESPN 150.

He decided to attend top Division I school University of Southern California, where he backed for the star quarterback. He thought once the quarterback left it would be his time to shine. But the starting quarterback didn't leave that year. . . or the next. Then, after two years of waiting, Max finally got to play in a collegiate game. This was his first time in the limelight since high school, his chance to prove to everyone just how good he had gotten while waiting on the bench.

Unfortunately, when the time came, it was a tough game that left USC with a devastating loss. After putting in years of work behind the scenes, the coach told Max he was being pulled from the starting lineup and they were going with the other backup quarterback instead.

Max refused to let his NFL dream die there. He was determined to still make it, even if it wasn't at USC. He transferred the following season to the University of Pittsburgh. He trained in the background again and came out as their new starting quarterback. Shortly into the season, he faced a career-ending shoulder injury.

In an athlete's career, there is no way to predict what will happen. Max had the skills and talent to perform in the NFL, but his path never led him to a place where he was able to showcase his abilities. This is true for many athletes. Less than five percent of DI men's baseball, football, basketball, and hockey players make it to the professional league, with even lower numbers in smaller sports and women's teams. No matter how hard an athlete trains, no matter how much time and energy he or she puts into it, there are some things that will always be out of their control. It hurts to let go of something that has been a constant in their life for so long.

> It hurts to let go of something that has been a constant in their life for so long.

Max recently spoke about his sports career on his girlfriend's podcast. In the episode, Max says, "I was on top of the world at seventeen; I was the number one quarterback in the country. I'd won every award, everyone was saying how great I was, everyone was kind of kissing my ass, but I never bought into that. My ego was never attached to what they were saying, I never got caught up in that hype. I always tried to stay grounded."

At an early age, Max was used to hearing praise for his football abilities. After a big win or new achievement, athletes find pride in their accomplishments. Especially when things are going well, it can be empowering and motivating for an athlete to be all-encompassed by their sport. But when performance isn't going well or an athlete's career is coming to an end, it can do more harm than good to stay attached to that identity.

When talking about the end of his career, Max recalled, "My identity at that stage was completely tied to football, but then I got to a point where I wasn't having success, and I wasn't happy. I wasn't having a good time. And then I learned this isn't fun, this isn't healthy, I shouldn't be wired this way."

Luckily for Max, he was able to ease his transition by keeping his athletic dreams and notoriety as a top recruit separate from how he saw himself. It can be easy to confuse competitive accomplishments with an athlete's identity. When athletes spend so long working towards a goal, whether they make it or not, it's an ingrained part of them. It's so deeply rooted in who athletes are that often we don't say "athletes *play* a sport," but "they *are* athletes."

Athletes aren't the only ones who find their worth in their work. It's a growing problem for adults in any field. Jeffrey Davis, M.A., wrote an article for Psychology Today called *You Are Not Your Work*. He described the problem:

"When you are told, again and again, that *you are your work*, you start to believe it. The trap in workism is associating your full identity and self-worth with your work, occupation, or job. You are not your work. Your work is simply a part of you. But it's difficult to separate the idea of meaningful work from a meaningful life."

I've heard a lot of athletes say that they feel like they no longer have a purpose after athletics. But athletes don't lose their meaningful

> When you are told, again and again, that you are your work, you start to believe it.

life after sports are over, they just lose the avenue through which they pursued meaningful work. "They are so passionate about their sport. and they're all in. They can only envision a career in soccer. They can only envision a career in football," Max continued. "But if you have that passion, couple it with self-awareness to know that your life has other chapters, other things are out there if you have that passion. You will be able to translate it to something else in life."

Max might not have become an NFL quarterback, but he is still passionate about the game. He's now a successful college football broadcaster and often shares his football story of how he failed his way to success. Although Max ended up finding a job he was passionate about, the first step when breaking an athletic identity isn't finding new meaningful work, which could lead to the same issues. The first step is turning inward.

INTERNAL IDENTITY:

Competing athletes can get so caught up in their current routine and goals that they aren't looking at what's next until it happens. They may get to retirement and think, "Who am I now?" This happened to swimmer Stephanie Rice. Stephanie Rice was an Australian swimmer and one of the best in the world. She won three gold medals at the 2008 Beijing Olympics and eagerly continued training for her chance at the next one. She made it to the London Olympics four years later, but due to an injury, she didn't perform as well and ultimately retired in 2012.

After she retired from swimming, she came to the same struggle that most athletes do, but often don't admit. Stephanie said on a podcast episode this year, "Everything that I knew about myself and prided myself on, and my confidence, came from swimming. So, take away the vehicle that gave me all of those feelings and all of that pride and confidence. It was like, 'Who is Stephanie Rice?', because I only knew Stephanie Rice as a swimmer."

Stephanie was in her twenties and didn't know what was coming. This is a common position for many people, but Stephanie spent her life up to that point training for swimming. When that was taken away, she felt as though the rug was pulled from under her. She struggled because for the first time in her life, she wasn't a swimmer. She took pride in her career and was confident in her ability in the pool. But outside the pool, she wasn't sure who she was and couldn't grasp who she would become.

She started to do deep reflections on who she was without her sport. Stephanie said, "This external gratification that I'm getting—medals, awards, money, and fame, are all amazing and I think everybody would like them. But they're also not true. They can come and go." Stephanie decided to dig deep and reflect on herself as a person. She came to terms with the fact that medals, awards, and fame are only temporary things. Not only are they temporary, but they're also something not in her control.

After reflecting on all the external things she thought made her who she was, she decided to focus inward. She said, "I need to focus my self-worth on things that I can control. Am I a good person? Do I feel like I'm contributing to something more than me? When I started really channeling into that, everything changed. That was a really big awakening. I thought, 'This is who I need to be and makes me feel the best.'"

STEP FOUR. E - EXPLORE YOUR IDENTITY:

To move on from sports you need to separate from your old athletic identity, especially when it's one that doesn't describe who you are anymore. In the study, *Retired Athletes and the Intersection of Food and Body,* researcher Georgina Buckley found, "Athletes who continued to engage in their athletic environments experienced heightened levels of objectification and were held back in their ability to re-identify. Continued involvement in the sport meant that those around them still perceived them as an athlete."

This is hard because it might be the first time you've been told this, and it's the opposite of what you've done in the past. Sports psychologist Dr. Caroline Silby said, "During your athletic career, it was beneficial to bury your head in your sport.

Transitioning is the opposite. You are reborn. Go connect with people. For the first time in your life, you will discover that your purpose is not tied to a stopwatch or scoreboard."

Maintaining an athletic identity will keep drawing you back to the past. To move forward you must let go. It's especially easy to look to the past when there's so much uncertainty in front of you. But, if you're stuck thinking about how things used to be, it will be hard to be hopeful for the future. You might feel stuck because being an athlete is all you've ever known, but here's another way to look at your life:

Your life

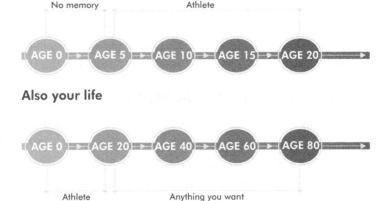

Also your life

If you have a yardstick of the life that you've lived, then it's easy to think that being an athlete is your whole identity. Looking back, you might have only known yourself as being an athlete and it's what you worked for your entire life. Since your earliest memories, you were playing catch or running down the soccer field and have kept it up ever since.

However, if you have a yardstick of your whole life, sports are only a small part of it. There is so much left of the yardstick that hasn't been lived yet. Sports might be all that you remember, but you don't even know what's in store for you in the future. Don't be afraid to lean into this unknown and lean into the unstructured.

Embrace the uncomfortable. Embrace the uncertainty that comes with freedom. I've called this phase the "messy middle" for a reason. It's supposed to feel new and messy. But out of that mess you're able to explore who you really are. You may still have that piece of athlete in you, but there's also so much more to you. Without your sport, you are not lacking, you're just different now. Different isn't bad, and change isn't bad. It just takes some adjustment.

Breaking your athletic identity is just the first step in moving forward. We attach our identity to the things we've done, not the things we've yet to do. There will come a time when you'll be past your athletic identity and wanting to find replacements. We'll explore next how to start structuring your new freedom.

* * *

For more tips on exploring your identity check out my podcast episode "Taking What You Learned in Sports into Life" at http://emilycoffman.org/taking-what-you-learned-in-sports-into-life/

CHAPTER 5:

LACING UP

———

"I love being strong. But I think there's so many different ways to be strong, and I don't limit myself to just being strong with a barbell anymore."

—INGRID MARCUM, USA BOBSLED AND USA WEIGHTLIFTING TEAM

It's time to get off the sidelines. Yes, a period of rest after athletics is normal, but it's time to get back in the game, no matter what that looks like. After competition is over it's clear that athletes struggle with how to keep showing up at the gym. Even though taking a break from working out is very common after retirement, I wondered what drew post-sport athletes back to exercising. I wanted to know if there was anything in common between the athletes who developed sustainable workout routines compared to the athletes that were never able to stick to a new one.

During my own journey, I struggled with this. Once I decided it was time for me to get back in shape, I joined a gym but found little motivation to go. This was hard to come to terms with because I thought, since I was an athlete for so long, I should have immediately enjoyed working out again, right?

I knew that it was time to get serious when I started to feel embarrassed telling others that I used to be an athlete. I started meeting new people in my city and job, and it would come up that I used to be a Division I Athlete, but that no longer resembled who I was. I couldn't remember the last time that I had gone to the gym. I couldn't even name any of the gyms in the area. I didn't like this new version of myself, so I knew that it was time to get off the sidelines and start working out again. But I didn't know where to start.

I found myself very lost at the gym. For years, I never once showed up to the gym questioning what workout I would do. I never had to question if I was ramping up my workouts or if I was doing too little or too much. This was all determined for me. I didn't know the first thing about creating a workout plan or how to use half of the equipment, but as a retired athlete, there was no way I was going to ask anyone at the gym for help. After having a gym membership for over six months and only successfully going a handful of times, I questioned if working out was something I'd ever find joy in again.

> I questioned if working out was something I'd ever find joy in again.

Later, a friend of mine recommended that I come to a group fitness class with her. I had no idea what that even meant, but I went and quickly realized that I had found my love for exercising again. In a group fitness class, I finally had an instructor telling me what to do again. I had a team around me whose energy I could feed off of. There was a clear goal at the end of class for which we were striving. Instantly, I found all the things I loved about sports in a cycling studio.

Starting to work out again after sports can feel over- whelming. Athletes spend years working towards one thing, and now there's no

> What does working out look like when the goal is no longer to finish first?

specific goal they're working towards. When starting to work out again, I had to ask myself: What does working out look like when the goal is no longer to finish first?

A NEED FOR CHANGE:

In almost every circumstance, an athlete's workout must change after retiring from competition. Either duration, intensity, or type has to adjust in order to meet the needs of the athlete's new lifestyle. This is especially true after dealing with an injury.

I spoke with one of my old high school teammates, Sarah Rapaport, about her transition out of athletics. Sarah was always an active person, and on top of rowing she had a love for running and marathons. She competed on the rowing team for Duke University but had a nagging injury that cost her the college athletic experience she hoped for. She was able to compete her freshman year, but after struggling with her injury on and off her sophomore year, she decided it was time to retire. Even though she was no longer rowing, the injury still affected her life afterward. It became too painful on her body to continue running as well.

Athletes find it hard to think of anything as a workout if it is less than pushing their bodies to the max. Since Sarah's body was no longer able to keep up with the same training, she had to change her outlook on what exercise really was. For former athletes, working out doesn't have to look like the training you did while competing. It boils down to the basic question of, "How can I move my body in a way that feels good?"

This was something Sarah struggled with too. She explained, "My mindset as an athlete, I had this expectation of myself that every time I was going to erg test [a fitness test on the indoor rowing machine], I was going to PR [Personal Record]. And I did it. But I think having that mindset in life doesn't set you up for happiness. Every time I PR'd I would be happy for a few minutes and then I'd be like, 'Now how can I shave off another ten seconds?'" She was constantly trying to improve and be her best which led to short bursts of shallow satisfaction.

Chris Smith, a former athlete from the University of Hawaii and current CEO of The Athlete Network explains it further. "As athletes, we are trained to constantly try to get better. We watch film and nitpick every mistake, looking for areas to constantly improve. If we enjoy our success or take our feet off the pedal, that's when we would lose as an athlete. I value most of the traits athletics has taught me, but this trait of 'good is never enough' needs to be checked and controlled."

Feeling the need to always improve in any aspect, but especially fitness, puts former athletes under unnecessary stress. A former athlete doesn't need to be at the same fitness level they were at while competing. The easiest way to get out of this mindset is to start celebrating the small wins. It's hard to do this while competing when an athlete's position is on the line, but after sport, there's no one to compete with besides oneself. Instead of celebrating when they hit a new personal best, athletes can redefine how they see working out. Not only does this set an athlete up to be more satisfied with their workouts, but it also sets them up to be happier in life.

Former elite gymnast Anja Garcia had a similar experience to Sarah's. Her gymnastics career was cut short during her junior year at UC Berkeley due to multiple injuries. She spent a year recovering from an ACL elbow reconstructive surgery but never was able to fully come back. She said, "Being injured and hurting every day just mentally took a toll on me. I ended up associating pain and suffering with the sport."

Earlier in her career, she made the decision to change her focus from the Olympics to a college scholarship due to her past injuries. This time, she had to make the decision to completely retire from gymnastics for good. Looking back, Anja has been able to see how this helped her out for life. She says now, "I try to see that though it's not the best ending in gymnastics, it was a better ending for the rest of my life."

After athletics, there needs to be some reflection on what an athletic career looks like compared to the rest of life. When the goal

> Though it's not the best ending in gymnastics, it was a better ending for the rest of my life.

for so long is being a top performer and an athlete's career gets cut short, it can be easy to be disappointed.

Luckily, the end of an athletic career doesn't have to mean the end of fitness. For Sarah, reframing what a workout looks like and changing her mindset to celebrate the smaller wins allowed her to create a successful life for herself after sport. When we discussed her exercise routine now, she said, "I try to do at least five miles every day of walking, which is funny to hear myself say because there was a time in my life when I wouldn't consider anything less than a ten-mile run or row a workout."

Similarly, Anja also didn't want her injury to keep her from fitness. She said, "When I quit, I thought I had to give up being an athlete. But now I know you are an athlete because you have a body." After retiring, she started teaching fitness classes in grad school and found that it brought her the same outlet that she had in gymnastics. She briefly stopped teaching because of her other job working as an ICU nurse, but she quickly realized how important it was for her to keep fitness in her life.

"I realized fitness and health are so much a part of the athlete in me that had never gone away, and I have to feed that part of me to be whole. When I teach that's the way I can do that." Both Anja and Sarah dealt with injuries that they have to be cognizant of even today. But by taking the focus off of performance and celebrating smaller wins they have been able to keep fitness in their lives.

NEW GOALS:

Athletes who come out of sports with an injury must change their perception of health and working out. But even non-injured athletes should change what working out looks like once they go back to the gym. Being in shape for competition looks different than being in shape for life, and training plans should change accordingly. There's no use in being able to outlift everyone in the gym if it's keeping you from other responsibilities or not leaving you with enough energy for your day.

There is a general assumption that athletes know how to be in shape because they have spent most of their lives doing so. Just because an athlete knows how and has done it before, doesn't mean they will continue to be active as their lifestyle changes. When they're a student and an athlete they have a lot of time to focus on their body, but when they replace a training schedule with a full-time, nine-to-five job, it's hard to continue fitting in the same workouts with a new lifestyle.

Not only do priorities change when you're no longer an athlete, but Dr. Reifsteck also argues that many athletes don't know how to train after sports. Reifsteck explains, "They know how to intensely train, but in many cases, they don't know as much about maintaining a healthy lifestyle."

A healthy lifestyle is much different than the lifestyle of a competing athlete. While there can be some similarities, an athlete doesn't need to mimic their old schedule to live a healthy lifestyle. Intense training is not needed daily, so it's important to learn that there can be (and should be) a place to fall in between complete rest and their previous athletic training schedule.

> They know how to intensely train, but in many cases, they don't know as much about maintaining a healthy lifestyle.

The goal for an athlete transitioning out of competition is to find a healthy, active lifestyle. This includes balance and rest along with physical activity and healthy eating. For many years of competition, athletes neglect balance and rest only to focus on their physical activity. Now that there's the freedom to choose, it's important for an athlete to find something sustainable that they enjoy doing to fit their current lifestyle. "Obviously, their lifestyle will shift," Dr. Reifsteck says. "We want to help them learn how to keep moving, stay active and eat healthfully without the constant supervision and structure of college athletics."

An athlete must learn how to do these things through exploration and trials of what fits in their new routine. There's a misconception from an athlete's perspective that they will automatically know how to do these things in their daily lives. However, an athlete is not always in the best mental and emotional space when leaving athletics. The potential increase in depression and anxiety can make things that seem simple, like staying active and eating well, even more difficult: especially, as Dr. Reifsteck mentioned, without any structure or guidance.

In another conversation I had with my former college teammate, Taylor Spencer, she talked about her struggles with working out after athletics. During college, Taylor was the definition of a dedicated athlete. She trained to her full potential during competition season and always went above and beyond doing extra workouts. When it came time for her to retire, she was already surrounded by many former athletes. She saw what their transition was like and decided she wanted to do her best to stay in her peak athletic shape.

She was in denial that she could possibly get out of peak shape. When we sat down to talk, she said, "The logic side of my brain knew that, but I didn't necessarily want to accept it. I think a part of me still was like, 'That was just their case, that doesn't have to be my case. I'm going to make sure that's not my case.'" Taylor knew it was a possibility for her to lose her performance and endurance but wasn't ready to accept it yet. Even after accepting a full-time job, she still tried to keep up her previous schedule by going to the gym every day, both before and after work.

After years of being evaluated on their body's performance, it's only natural for an athlete to want to keep that valued part of them from weakening. It seems like something that is in their control. So, even when they are no longer required to keep the performance up, many will try to in order to maintain their athletic identity. This leads back to why breaking the athletic identity is important for overall health and well-being.

Even though Taylor was pushing herself to go to the gym twice a day every day, the workouts were starting to feel different. She was used to pushing her body to its limits for rowing, and going to a gym didn't bring that same feeling. "I was working out, but I never felt truly accomplished because I couldn't reach that absolute death stage," she described. "I just never felt like what I was doing was enough."

A lot of athletes feel like they haven't accomplished something if they don't sense it in their bodies. In

> I just never felt like what I was doing was enough.

an interview with Athletes Soul, Rebecca Soni, a six-time swimming Olympic medalist, mentioned very similar feelings. She went from the highest level of swimming to sitting at a desk all day. She recalls, "For a long time I didn't feel like I did anything. I could have had a lot of successes in my work that day, but it didn't feel like it because I didn't wreck my body."

Most of her previous successes were all physical. She left races and competitions physically exhausted which indicated to her that she has succeeded. Both for Taylor and Rebecca, without leaving with their bodies physically feeling like they did after competition, it was hard to see their actions as accomplishments.

After a few months trying to keep up her intense workout schedule, Taylor realized she was no longer in the same shape. She tried to do the erg test that she had done many times before in her rowing career. This time, she felt the exhaustion hit a lot sooner than before. Taylor finally came to the realization that keeping up her physical capabilities would not be possible with her new lifestyle.

Even though this left her feeling defeated and frustrated, she still had the desire to continue having exercise in her life. She leaned on the other former athletes in her life who had also retired. She said, "They told me it's really important that you have a goal, either you're doing it for fun, or you have a goal that you're working towards. Because otherwise you're going to fall out of it. It just happens."

Now, instead of having the same goal from her rowing days, Taylor made new goals that wouldn't leave her feeling exhausted and frustrated. She tried CrossFit workouts with her boyfriend, new fitness apps, and a month-long running challenge with her friends. Looking back, she says, "Professional athletes—and to a degree, college athletes—get paid to be at their top physical fitness levels. So nobody's judging you for not maintaining that fitness level after graduating."

STEP FIVE. L - LOVE YOUR WORKOUT

Your new goal? Loving your workout.

Creating your own workout used to be a novelty. Now it's your reality! After having every season, competition, and workout planned for you to a tee, you now have the freedom to explore everything you never had the chance to try before.

OLD SCHEDULE

EVERYTHING
ELSE

NEW SCHEDULE

EVERYTHING
ELSE

The problem, however, is that you likely won't have the same amount of time in your new daily routine to dedicate to exercise. Before, practice and sleep accounted for most of your day. Now work, sleep, and errands will take up most of your day. However, even with this change, you can still make time to work out. It might be harder to prioritize, but athletes are known to have great time management skills.

There are a lot of ways to continue having exercise in your life that don't require the same intensity that you had in competitive sports. In fact, many professionals recommend trying activities that are different than the ones you did in sport.

In an interview from Cleveland Clinic with Dr. Carly Day, she discussed how someone can make the shift from being an athlete to becoming an active adult. Carly said, "What makes people strong athletes doesn't always serve their long-term well-being." For example, "Maximal lifting may make you stronger for football, but continuing extreme lifting into later life will likely cause orthopedic problems." Not only is it not practical to perform like you once did, but the later in your life you go, injuries can develop from that level of intense training.

Instead, try to change it up. Try a new activity that you haven't tried before or you weren't able to do while competing. Find fitness in your everyday life that doesn't involve going to the gym. You can try rollerblading or bike riding to spend time outdoors after spending most of your day in an office. You can find recreational leagues or fun charity tournaments. Find fitness that fits your new lifestyle.

> Find fitness that fits your new lifestyle.

Some athletes get stuck in the same exercise routine because it's all they know. It's just easier for some to continue what they were doing instead of learning something new. But no one is meant to be a high performing athlete forever, and bodies can't sustain that intensity forever. Many athletes leave sports feeling burnt out, and going back to the same workouts can leave them getting burnt out again. As Taylor and many others figured out, there has to be a shift in your workouts in order to be sustainable after sports.

Now that we've broken your mindset around the rules you had about exercise, let's look into what food rules you're still holding onto.

* * *

If you need further guidance on creating a workout plan you love, check out my podcast episode "Three Steps to Enjoy Your Workout" at emilycoffman.org/three-steps-to-enjoy-your-workout/

CHAPTER 6:

BREAKING FOOD RULES

———

"Nutrition can be confusing, and to simplify things, it can seem easy or even comforting to have black and white food rules to follow. But the truth is, food rules set people up for failure and ultimately do nothing to help you gain a healthy, balanced diet."

—NICOLA JACKSON, NUTRITIONIST

We're told a lot of things that we take to be the truth in sports. Like, if you're not first, you're last. There's no "I" in team. And that there is a certain way we should eat. Sometimes these things aren't told to us directly, but they surround us. When we see our teammates trying to lose weight, or our competitors claiming that a certain diet is what led to their new success, athletes can think that these things are the answer.

I remember every year of school taking nutrition classes or, as they called it in middle school, "home ed." They taught us how sugar and sweets were bad and how you need to have a vegetable at every meal. I then became a college athlete, and the team dietitian repeated the mantra of how sugar and sweets were bad and to have a vegetable at every meal.

At one of our monthly lectures with the dietitian, I remember her standing in the front of the lecture hall with a baggie full of sugar. She waved the baggie to everyone in the front row and asked, "Did you know this is the amount of sugar in every soda you drink?!" A bag full of sugar is equivalent to a cup of soda. Note to self: no soda.

They would lecture us on how sugary desserts should only be consumed in the thirty-minute window after working out so it would be used as energy. Starbucks' drinks are just liquid calories stored as fat. Coffee will dehydrate you, sugar will keep you awake, and let's not forget how one sip of alcohol will slow down your training by one week. Note to self: no desserts, Starbucks, or alcohol.

I only came to realize after leaving sports that I wasn't actually learning about nutrition. I was learning which foods were good, which foods were bad, and what rules I had to follow. These were fed to us through the mask of "you will do whatever it takes to be great." And as athletes, we did!

DISORDERED EATING:

Food rules are something that athletes not only learn over time but are also taught at a very young age. I was listening to a podcast interview with former athlete Georgie Buckley. She was an elite-level track and field distance runner in Australia. From a young age, she was naturally good at running and became a Junior National Champion in high school. At only thirteen years old, she was already hearing negative comments about her body changes.

"Coaches or other athletes talked about girls going through puberty as a very unfavorable thing," she recalled on the *Nail*

Your Nutrition podcast. "The belief that was engrained amongst us was as soon as you hit puberty, you'll run badly for two to three years, and if you make it out of that, you'll be fine." Georgie equated hitting puberty with weight gain and slower times. She heard this from coaches and teammates and believed this wholeheartedly since she hadn't heard another point of view. She learned that body changes were negative but never learned about eating disorders.

At the time she didn't see anything wrong with her eating habits. She thought if she saw her teammates and others doing it, then it

> They taught her that body changes were negative and never taught her about eating disorders.

must not be that bad. Georgie said, "It's not a surprise that when female athletes' bodies are commented on it pushes them to a place of disconnected eating. They might not identify as having disordered eating because that's what their coach told them to do, that's what their teammates do." Most athletes aren't taught about the nutrition behind how to eat. They're only taught food rules or that they need to lose weight, and food is what will get them there by following more rules, not learning better nutrition.

After going through puberty and having her body change, it didn't get better for Georgie. In the world of distance running, race weight is a common term that is thrown around. It's referring to the weight at which a runner best performs. Most of the time, this is also the smallest weight a runner can maintain. Georgie says, "And we think that [race weight] is what I need to be at and we're coming up to a big race, and we're not that. What are we going to do? We're going to restrict our food." Just like Georgie had seen her puberty and race weight as good versus bad, this often carries over into athletes' food choices too. Too much food causes weight gain so it must be bad. This leads to very unhealthy relationships between athletes and food.

Georgie said that due to her food restriction before races, she would binge for weeks after the season was over. She stated, "I can now look back and say that because I was restricting so much in the lead up to these big races, that the aftermath was that binge, and I think often people normalize this."

> It's seen as yet another sacrifice athletes make for their sport.

Disordered eating like this is very normalized in sport. It's seen as yet another sacrifice athletes make for their sport. But this sacrifice isn't healthy or helping. When something like unhealthy eating is all around you and so normalized in sport, it's hard to see disordered eating as a big problem. But now, looking back, Georgie sees how engrained it was in her career. This disordered eating looked so much like her being a dedicated athlete that Georgie's mom even commented years later: "I'm really surprised you never developed an eating disorder given your personality traits."

Georgie isn't alone in feeling like disordered eating was all around her. It's extremely common for athletes to have disordered relationships with food and exercise. According to the National Eating Disorders Association, it is estimated that disordered eating affects 62 percent of female athletes and 33 percent of male athletes. This isn't a few cases. This is affecting a large percentage of male athletes and most female athletes.

After Georgie left running, she went on to become a dietitian. She learned about disordered eating and realized that these were the habits she saw as an athlete. She describes disordered eating as a very hard thing to define because it's not defined by an athlete's actions, but by their mentality and intention behind their actions. "Disordered eating is the umbrella. And then under that we have our thoughts, and then our behaviors. People think of disordered eating as just the obvious behaviors."

CHANGING EATING BEHAVIORS:

On the other side of the spectrum are the athletes who put little thought into their nutrition. There are so many other performance factors to pay attention to that what they're eating just isn't as important. An athlete's criteria for good nutrition may be that if they are energized enough for practice and whatever they eat doesn't change the way they look, then they're good.

I was speaking to one of my friends and fellow former collegiate athletes, Rich Chapman, about his transition out of basketball and what his nutrition was like. He described his eating during competition. "In college, I would just eat a ton. We would go get dinner after working out, and instead of a sandwich and a side I would get two sandwiches and eat them both. I would try to minimize things like sugars and unhealthy fats and carbs as much as possible, but I was still just eating a lot of food." Due to the volume of working out, nutrition wasn't thought about nearly as much as trying to fuel for games and practice.

"When I worked out for basketball I felt like a black hole of hunger and nothing could ever fill me up," Rich recalled. With the constant need to be refueling, athletes will often choose convenient options which might not correlate to the healthiest options.

> With the constant need to be refueling, athletes will often choose convenient options which might not correlate to the healthiest options.

A few years removed from sport, Rich's nutrition now looks different, but he's still motivated to stay healthy. After graduating, he moved to the small island of Sitka, Alaska, without any connection but his job. "They had one gym, which was actually a pretty nice gym for a town of eight thousand people, and I had a lot of downtime to myself. So, I lifted a lot of weights, did as little cardio as I could, and tried to get as strong and big as I could." Basketball was no longer an option to him, but staying in shape was. He was able to continue working on himself and his health, even without sports.

Nutrition is a part of staying in shape, even if current athletes don't see it that way. Rich finds it even easier to stay healthy now. "I always feel that the more I work out the hungrier I get. So, I found it easier when I'm not working out as often to eat better since I don't have to eat as much," Rich says. "Now I can throw together a little bit of chicken and some rice and that's a good meal. But if I was playing basketball, or had a game, I would need chicken, rice, and a cheeseburger to fill me up." Since the amount of food a former athlete eats is less than what was needed for competition, it can be easier to fit in healthier foods. Former athletes also don't always have to choose the most convenient option anymore since they don't have to eat between games, travel, and everything else on their schedule.

> The 'I'll just burn it off' mentality is a set-up for failure.

Katie Hargrave, a holistic health coach and personal trainer, similarly wrote about nutrition and an athlete's mentality around it in her book *The Athlete After*. She said, "Just because you can eat it and not gain weight, doesn't mean that it is good for you, fueling you properly, and helping you to perform the best you can. The 'I'll just burn it off' mentality is a set-up for failure—not only does everything you put in your mouth affect you at a cellular level, but it's also allowing you to develop horrible habits that stick with you once you stop working out constantly." Although eating whatever you want while competing might have been fine, it sets an athlete up to have bad habits. What is one thing bad habits and food rules have in common? We need to break them!

STEP SIX. I - IMPROVE NUTRITION KNOWLEDGE:

In order to break out of the "I'll just burn it off" mentality and un-supported food rules, you must improve your nutrition knowledge. Knowledge relaxes rules. The more learning you do on nutritional facts, the more you can evaluate your eating and the rules that you've been following. By educating yourself on food and nutrition, you can be confident that you're able to adapt to whatever your new goals and training look like. No more doing the same old thing just because that's what worked in the past.

In the past your primary goal was athletic performance. As athletes, we may assume that the fastest or strongest athletes must also be the healthiest for getting there, right? Wrong. Performance is only a sliver of our overall health. Health is made up of our physical, mental, and social health. Physical health is then broken into how you move, eat, sleep, and how you take care of your body. Fitness level can be based off endurance, strength, balance, and flexibility. As a result, performance is how you execute your fitness level at a specific point in time.

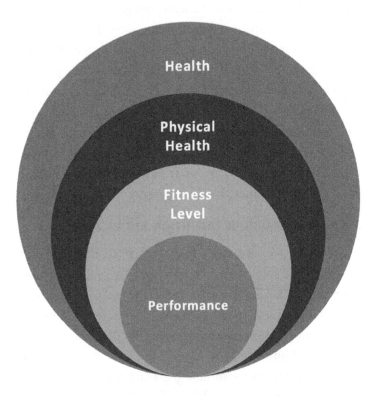

As an athlete, I'm sure you've prioritized performance over your health many times, putting competitions ahead of your sleep, nutrition, or mental health. Well, in your new routine, your priorities should look different. The main focus should be on overall health and equally evaluating where you are physically, mentally, and socially. If that feels balanced, then you can move on to improving your physical health and making sure that fitness is no longer superior to nutrition. After that, you can improve fitness levels and performance, but not at the cost of the first steps of overall health.

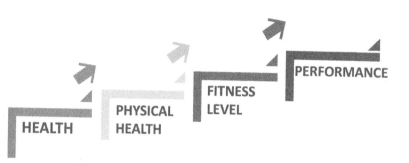

By making your health a gradual step, you can improve at whatever speed you want. You will no longer try to aim towards performance while disregarding the building blocks that help you get there. The more you educate yourself on nutrition, the less likely it is that you'll trap yourself in a mind-set of "performance over everything."

Now that you've done the work of breaking your limiting beliefs, you can make your way out of the messy middle. You've changed how you approach working out, eating, and your past identity. Now, you can focus on the better days ahead. Let's look at how to use this new knowledge to successfully become your best self as an everyday athlete.

* * *

All mentioned resources, along with clips of my conversation with Rich Chapman, can be found at emilycoffman.org/bookresources

PHASE THREE: BETTER DAYS AHEAD

CHAPTER 7:

BE A CAMO

———

"I love to compete. I love to teach, to lead and to be a part of a team. And so, to be in a position where I can use all those things on a day-to-day basis and focus all my energy on those tenets is a perfect fit."

—STEVE NASH, HALL OF FAME BASKETBALL PLAYER, CURRENT NBA COAC

———

So, what is an everyday athlete? I define it as a noun—someone who stays active and healthy for everyday life instead of for a competition or job. After competing, a former athlete doesn't lose an athletic identity forever. Instead, they become an everyday athlete. Everyday athletes can keep sports in their lives through participation in sports or becoming a coach, mentor, or spectator of the sport.

FEELING FULFILLED:

I sat down with Bethany Hart Gerry, an Olympic bobsledder and elite-level hammer thrower—an event where a metal ball attached to a grip is thrown for distance. After the Olympics, she retired from both sports and realized she no longer had the drive to continue working out if there wasn't an Olympic goal at the end. When trying to figure out what to do next she said, "I couldn't go back to semblances of my sports, because I didn't feel like I was going to ever be able to attain the level I did."

For the athletes who aren't burnt out of their sport by retirement, it's still hard for them to continue training the same way. Athletes naturally won't be able to continue performing at the same level they did when competing, which can be discouraging. Instead, Bethany decided to try something similar but different from what she had done in her past.

CrossFit intrigued her since it had a huge community behind it and many of her personal trainer friends recommended it. She joined a CrossFit gym and realized this was something she'd be able to stick with. "I think what CrossFit did for me was still let me push my body to the limits. I learned new skills and a new way to condition my body." She found CrossFit fun because it had the element of competition but required completely different skills than what she had trained for before. This brought out the same competitiveness she had for bobsledding. and she went on to compete in the CrossFit games both regionally and nationally. Bethany knew that competition was her motivation, and just because the Olympics were no longer a goal didn't mean she couldn't find a new competitive scene.

Sometimes athletes just need competition in their lives to stay motivated.

In a study called *Why do people like competition?* researcher Robert Franken said, "We hypothesized that people who are motivated by competition are motivated for at least three reasons: competition allows them to satisfy the need to win, competition provides the opportunity or reason for improving their performance, and competition motivates them to put forth greater effort that can result in high levels of performance." Sometimes athletes just need competition in their lives to stay motivated.

Competition was engrained in Bethany from a young age and wasn't something she wanted to give up. The good news is that Bethany, like any other former athlete, didn't need to abandon this. There are ways to continue being an athlete without needing to compete at the highest level. An elite athlete can become an everyday athlete.

AN EVERYDAY ATHLETE:

Another athlete I spoke with, Katherine Kulhman, shared a similar story when discussing how she found her workout routine. She was a Division I swimmer in college and loved the feeling of being in a pool. When talking about the training she said, "You jump in a pool, you're by yourself, and you can't hear anything. You're staring at a blank line, and there's something really therapeutic about being in your own world in that sense." It wasn't the competition that she missed, but the meditative feeling she got while being in a pool. The feeling of being "in the zone."

After college, she moved for a job in Tanzania where she didn't have access to any pools. She tried picking up running and training for a half marathon but found that wasn't fulfilling for her. Swimming was a huge mental relief for Katherine; without a pool, she was missing her outlet. "There is something really special about being able to be in your own head for two hours, and it's really difficult once you lose it," she reflects. Katherine wasn't able to continue swimming, but she wanted another outlet.

After the half marathon training, she called it quits on running but concluded that she did enjoy the time she got to spend outside. She started routinely going for walks which was the perfect mix of moving her body and having the same therapeutic results as swimming. Because walking was able to fill the void that swimming had left as a mental outlet, Katherine found it easier to keep up with her daily walks and started to miss swimming less.

It's no surprise then why we see so many professional athletes from other sports transition to golf once they're done competing. They're replacing what they loved about their old sport to a less physically demanding one where they can still feel fulfilled. I was listening to an interview the other day by Golf.com featuring Tony Romo, a former NFL quarterback who played on the Dallas Cowboys for fourteen seasons. After football, he picked up golf—not just as a weekend hobby, but as something that he practiced for up to six to eight hours some days. Romo said, "I just liked competition, at its core. As a kid, I wanted to grow up and play sports in some fashion."

After he left the NFL his drive to continue competing didn't go away. Romo liked how sports gave him the ability to continuously improve. It wasn't that he was going to miss running around a field, but that he was going to miss the ability to practice and improve on something every day. "I think it's the puzzle aspect, it's no different than me trying to figure out the throwing motion." When he was in the NFL, he liked being able to fine-tune a skill every day. As he got older, he wasn't able to keep up in football, but he could transfer that same mindset to golf.

Romo said, "I used to have pure joy going to bed at night thinking that I got better, and that the next day you're finally going to see the real version of what you always wanted to be."

STEP SEVEN. N – NURTURE A NEW ATHLETIC ROLE:

Experts who work with former athletes have seen a lot of success in their mental and physical health when athletes stay involved in sports. I spoke with sports psychologist Dr. Mitch Greene, and he noted that athletes tend to do a lot better with the transition when they find ways to remain active in athletics. He said that multiple athletes he's worked with found their way back to sports because they felt like a part of them was missing. Mitch shared a story with me of one athlete who competed as a runner and after retiring decided to pick up weightlifting. Mitch said, "He's still got a connection to running because he coaches some people, but he's also got a connection to a whole new world of people in the world of weightlifting and bodybuilding that I think has made his life feel more complete."

Keeping sports in your life can help with working out again or just feeling fulfilled. But staying an active athlete is just one of the ways to keep sports in your life. Let's break down the others into what I call "CAMO."

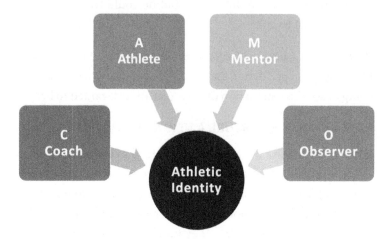

C- Coach

A - Athlete

M - Mentor

O - Observer

COACH:

Every coach at some point used to be an athlete. Former athletes already have a background in the sport, have developed different skills and strategies, and have a love for the game. This makes it a no-brainer why so many athletes then go on to become coaches. Grant Goldschmidt, a former South African volleyball player, is now a coaching lecturer at ETA College in South Africa. He wrote an article about the different benefits former athletes notice when becoming coaches after retirement.

Grant states, "If you love sport, why not develop a career in sport? Over the years of being a pro athlete, I have borne witness to so many other athletes and sport fanatics who become ensnared in careers that they do not want to be in. . . . Being a coach allows you to stay involved in sport in some way and dedicate your life to something you love and have a passion for."

If you have a passion for sports, no one is saying you have to find that passion somewhere else. You

---

If you love sport, why not develop a career in sport?

---

can still find it in sports, but maybe a different way! Coaching provides an opportunity to stay close to the sport but by helping others reach the same athletic goals you once were going after. Just like you don't need to compete at the highest level possible, you also don't need to coach at an elite level to be successful. You can find yourself a full-time coaching position or do it part-time for a less competitive league. Either way, if sports is something you enjoyed, you might find that same fulfillment by helping others reach their athletic goals.

MENTOR:

Another way to stay involved in sports is to become a mentor to a current athlete. There are programs that formally do this, or you could informally be a mentor to a former teammate or someone from your former team. Mentorship has proven to help athletes transition to life after sport because it allows them to reflect on their time as an athlete.

A mentorship program in Canada called Athlete Transitions found that "many athletes report that taking on a mentorship role themselves was beneficial in the redefining of their own identities. The process of helping others allowed them to explore parts of their personality they had not previously explored and offered new insights into their own athletic experiences and how they could be utilized in their new post-sport lives." Being a mentor can help you think back to your sports experience with a new lens. We often think of our careers as how they ended, but when talking through your experience with a current athlete you're able to process all the other aspects of what made you an athlete too.

Think about ways you could be a mentor. Would you be interested in elementary, middle, or high school? Would you want the mentorship to be formal or informal? Being a mentor could keep sports in your life just like being a coach, but without the pressure of statistics and athletic performance. Mentorship might be the thing for you if you're looking to use your expertise and experience to make an impact in an athlete's life outside of the game.

OBSERVER:

While being a coach or mentor is a large time commitment, almost all athletes I know become an observer in their post-sport life. Being a spectator or sports fan can make you feel just as connected to the game as you were before retirement.

Psychologists who studied sports fans found that there were eight reasons people liked watching sports. Some of the reasons included, "People like sports because they get self-esteem benefits from it. People like sports because it's exciting. People like sports because it's aesthetically pleasing. People like sports because, like the theater, it is a venue for emotional expression. People like sports because they need an escape from real-world troubles. People like sports because it provides a sense of belonging, a connection to a wider world." Watching sports isn't just a pastime like watching Netflix, it's a way for you to feel connected to a team, get an escape, and be entertained.

Plus, as an observer, you're allowed to be a fair-weather fan. No commitments here!

Whether you're interested in being a coach, athlete, mentor, or observer, there remains a place in athletics for you. Staying involved can help you feel fulfilled just like competition did for so many years. Don't lose your athletic identity entirely, just be a CAMO. Being a CAMO will allow you to find new things to enjoy, but let's see how else you can spend your new free time.

* * *

For free tips and motivation on becoming an everyday athlete, subscribe on YouTube at emilycoffman.org/youtube

CHAPTER 8:

BROADENING YOUR PLAYBOOK

———

"As we grow up in sports, we belong. We are not outsiders because for most of us, being on a sports team provides a place where we can truly feel like ourselves. Everyone is like us. They are all on the same schedule, eat the same food at training table, wear the same sweats and talk about the same things. This is our normal, and this is all we know."

—*KELLI TENNANT, WOMEN'S VOLLEYBALL PLAYER*

The best part of athletic retirement is one that athletes crave during their competition days: all the free time! Yes, they might be going on to start a new career, further their education, or start something new, but 6 a.m. and weekends will now be theirs again. It's easy to use all this time for rest but, as covered in chapter two, rest should only be one component. Now that there's more free time, an athlete should spend this freedom trying new things.

When I retired, I tried a lot of different activities. I saw my family more, took more road trips, and spent time jumping into different group fitness classes. All these things were great and made me happy, but they also left me stuck where I was. I was enjoying life, but I wasn't growing. What helped move me forward wasn't filling my time more, it was stepping outside of my comfort zone.

About two years after retiring, I had the idea I wanted to start a podcast. I had no idea what it really meant to host a podcast and didn't know anyone personally who created one, but it sounded exciting and I wanted a place to share my story and connect with others. It took courage to open up about my athletic journey with others and hear myself on a recording. I had never done any public speaking, so putting my thoughts into the world without knowing who would listen at first was scary. When I put myself out there for sports, I did it because I knew I was good at it. Podcasting . . . not so much.

But pushing myself out of my comfort zone was worth it. One year later and the *Live Your Personal Best* podcast has reached over 200,000 people and has given me a new project. Just like in sports, in podcasting there was always more to learn and improve upon. I now have a lot of skills to work on that I've never needed before. I'm learning how to be better at interviewing, storytelling, marketing, and building an audience. It also gave me the structure that I was missing from competition.

We need a place of productive discomfort.

Podcasting was the perfect balance of something that I knew nothing about but a manageable task to learn.

Author of *Drive* Daniel Pink said, "We need a place of productive discomfort, if you're too comfortable, you're not productive. And if you're too uncomfortable, you're not productive. Like Goldilocks, we can't be too hot or too cold." To be most productive, an athlete has to push outside their comfort zone.

CHANGE IT UP:

One of my friends from college had a slightly different approach to leaving her comfort zone. My friend, Brenna Dowell, was a fellow Division I Athlete with me at OU and was a member of the women's gymnastics team. She came to college after training on the National team for the Olympics and was used to an elite level of training from a very young age. Brenna didn't realize how much sports impacted her entire day until after retiring. When I spoke to her on retirement, she recalled, "You would literally wake up in the morning and do your whole day knowing you had practice that day. You think, 'I can't eat this, or I can't do that, it might make me tired.'"

Brenna said that she would plan her whole day around how she would feel for practice even though it wouldn't happen until the end of her day. When she stopped practicing for competition she says, "It was a weight that was lifted off my shoulders that I didn't realize that I was carrying." She no longer had this burden. Even when an athlete is not at practice, they still have to plan out their days and meals and structure everything around their training.

Now that she no longer had practice, she was excited for what could take its place. Brenna said, "I was ready to be able to do all

> It was a weight that was lifted off my shoulders that I didn't realize that I was carrying.

the things I had to miss out on because I was in gymnastics. I had to choose softball or gymnastics when I was eight years old, so it was basically all I've done my whole life."

Athletes usually pick up their sports from a very young age. This is the only schedule and identity they know. Now that it was over, Brenna was excited to travel, a hobby previously only available to her through competition. The summer after she retired, she studied abroad in Europe for two months. During her trip, she was able to eat and move her body however she wanted without thinking about her sport.

Brenna believes this big shift helped her have an easier transition out of sports. She said, "After I finished, it wasn't like I missed gymnastics and was going through my daily routine but didn't have to go to practice. It was a completely new daily routine." I'm not saying that every athlete should travel for two months after retirement, although I would never suggest against it . . . but change up your routine. Brenna said that she wasn't thinking about what her old teammates were doing at practice or what she normally would be doing at that time. She was too busy making new memories.

Once an athlete stops competing, it can be a scary and uncertain time with all the freedom and lack of structure. An athlete can stay in the fear or choose to focus on the positives and think about using this time to try something new.

Comfort is a good place to go back to, but not to stay put forever.

Luckily, if there's anyone who would be best at this, it is a former athlete. Athletes are used to living outside their comfort zones. Every practice and competition they try to push their limits and experiment with how to get to that next level. This is something that athletes are naturally doing, but without the pressure to perform, they might fall back to a place of comfort. Comfort is a good place to go back to, but not to stay put forever.

TRYING SOMETHING NEW:

Another athlete who pushed himself out of his comfort zone and into a new venture was former NFL quarterback Drew Bledsoe. After retiring from football, he knew he needed to find something else to fill his time and become his new passion and purpose.

"The biggest thing the successful [retired athletes] had in common was they had something to throw themselves into—a place to apply the passion that it took to play a sport," Drew said in an interview with Boston.com. "You leave one career at a young age and doing nothing is a recipe for disaster. That was a big motivator behind wanting to start a business."

He had seen many of his old teammates retire before him. Some were more successful than others and the successful ones had something in common: they moved onto something new. Drew moved back to his hometown and started running a winery. It wasn't something in which he had any prior experience, but it was something he wanted to learn more about. In a separate interview with ESPN, Drew said, "I was successful as a football player. Can I start over at something totally different and become successful at that too?"

> The successful ones had something in common: they moved onto something new.

After competition athletes have to face the obstacle of trying something new. Even though it's a new playing field, there will always be similarities in sports and in life. It's not about starting over; it's about finding what an athlete loved about their sport and applying it somewhere else. After starting his new business Drew found that it was a lot more like football than he originally thought.

"You got to plan and plan and plan," Drew told Boston.com. "In football, you're always game-planning all offseason and every week leading up to a game. Then you go try to execute that plan on Sunday. It's the same in business. You're just planning and planning and planning and preparing to execute your plan." Even though Drew was outside of his comfort zone when starting a winery, he was confident because it was building on the success he had as an athlete.

Others close to Drew also noticed how the shift he made into a new field helped him with the transition. "Merely starting a wine business helped ease Bledsoe out of the locker room. He admits it would have been difficult otherwise," the interviewers noted. "The sport he'd built his life around since childhood had left a football-sized hole. But Bledsoe is also preternaturally competitive. Only when the critical and commercial success of his wines was assured was he able to put his playing career, the business finished and unfinished, safely in the past."

Just like Drew found a new hobby and Brenna drastically changed up her routine, the transition will look different for all athletes. Leaving sports isn't easy, but it is possible to come out seeing the grass is greener. The only thing stopping an athlete is the unknown. They can't know what they'll enjoy next if they haven't tried anything but sports, so it's important to use this freedom to explore. Not all of them will stick, but eventually one of them will.

STEP EIGHT. E - EXPAND YOUR COMFORT ZONE:

If you're looking to find your next passion, it likely won't come from the things you're already doing. Passive comes from your comfort zone. Passion comes from action.

Recently, Yale neuroscientists conducted a study proving that uncertainty helps us learn. It was found, "One implication of the findings, according to Lee, is that we should seek out new situations to stimulate brain activity and learn more." When entering a new phase in life, a lot of learning is required, and in order to best learn, we should step outside our comfort zone. Just like learning a new skill in your sport, passion comes from doing something unfamiliar.

Sticking with what feels familiar may help you short-term, but it'll hurt in the long-term. Researchers also found that leaving

> Many of us are like lions in the zoo: well-fed but sit around passively stuck in a reactive rut.

your comfort zone helps increase your motivation to exceed in life. *Psychology Today* author Ran Zilca says, "Comfort reduces our motivation for introducing important transformations in our lives. Sadly, being comfortable often prohibits us from chasing our dreams. Many of us are like lions in the zoo: well-fed but sit around passively stuck in a reactive rut. Comfort equals boring shortsightedness, and a belief that things cannot change."

This bears repeating: comfort reduces our motivation for introducing important transformations. In this case, if you feel comfortable staying a "former athlete," then you won't feel motivated to keep moving forward. It doesn't have to start as big as starting a new business. In fact, wine wasn't even Drew's first venture out of sports. He dipped his toe in oil, gas, and coffee too. But you can start small. Think, "What is one thing today that could break me out of my comfort zone?" This could be changing up your order at your usual dining spot. Or, thinking through a decision when you're usually quick to act. Or, signing up for a networking event. The list can go on for whatever activities come up in your day.

In fact, it will be easier if you start small. Andy Molinsky, author of *Reach: A New Strategy to Help You Step Outside Your Comfort Zone, Rise to the Challenge and Build Confidence,* said in an interview, "You might be afraid that other people will see you as not good at it. So, it's not only the anxiety of being not so good at it, but also the fear and embarrassment and potentially shame of knowing that your incompetence is pretty visible."

The fear that comes with stepping outside of your comfort zone is because you won't be good at it yet. You may have heard from coaches something along the lines of "temporary discomfort leads to permanent improvement," and the same is true here. Temporarily, you may feel outside your comfort zone, but after that initial step, every time you move forward, it will become more and more familiar.

Finding your passion after sports is linked directly to one thing: going outside your comfort zone. If you don't try new things, you'll never know what's out there! It might be easier to stay in recovery mode of life and passively sit on the bench, but you were made for more. Now that you're exploring your next passion, there's one final step in how to go from finding this passion to turning it into part of your new life.

* * *

For more tips on trying something new, check out my podcast episode "10 Steps to Breaking Out of Your Comfort Zone" at emilycoffman.org/jumpstartyourlife

CHAPTER 9:

PLAYING THE GAME OF LIFE

"[Sports] was a job where 'good' was never 'good enough.' You were always trying to improve and get better. It was a job that if you acted like you were satisfied, you were fired or someone else came along and took your spot."

—*CHRIS SMITH, CEO OF THE ATHLETE NETWORK, DIVISION I CENTER*

Ambition is a common trait in athletes. They dream of going to the Olympics, winning championships, and beating records. For years athletes push themselves and their bodies to the limits and want to be the best. Athletes are known to be driven and hardworking, but when the competitions end and the goals become fuzzy, they lose that sense of belonging.

The typical next thing to do is try to find a new thing to be the best at. Athletes are great at competing, and they go back to what they know. After excelling in one area of their life,

> Sports are about winning; life is about enjoying. .

athletes might be surprised to find out what it feels like to be a beginner again.

Sports are about winning; life is about enjoying. There are bigger and better things ahead. Happiness comes from more than winning a gold medal, and success is measured by more than just accomplishments. The goal is to enjoy whatever comes next, and the easiest way to move on is to create a new identity.

STARTING OVER:

Kobe Bryant had arguably the best basketball career he could've worked for. He broke many records, won five NBA championships, two Olympic Gold Medals, and was inducted into the Hall of Fame. Once he retired, he had his sight set on his future career plans. In an interview after his retirement, he said, "Focus on what is ahead, and it takes a lot of bravery to be able to do that, because what if that falls flat, then what? It is always easier to go with what is. But that ain't what we do. We push forward, and that is the biggest challenge ahead."

Kobe was so successful in his basketball career and could've called that his one career, but he wanted more than that. It might have been easier to cling onto basketball, but he was up for the challenge of learning something new and moving to the next thing in his life. Later in the interview, he said, "Fast-forward twenty years from now: if basketball is the best thing I've done in my life, then I've failed. It's a very simple mission, very simple quest, very simple goal. These next twenty years need to be better than the previous twenty."

Kobe didn't say this because he wasn't proud of his basketball career or accomplishments. He said this because he knew that

there was still more pas-
sion in him that he wanted
to explore. The ambition
an athlete has doesn't go
away just because they are
no longer competing. Kobe

> It's a very simple mission, very simple quest, very simple goal. These next twenty years need to be better than the previous twenty.

took the skills and passion he had in sports and transferred
them to the next stage in his life.

An athlete instinctively has drive, but once retired might not
have an outlet for this anymore. Former football player Darryll Stinson went through this same stage in his transition of
wondering how he could use his skills somewhere else. Darryll
was a college football player who had big dreams of going to
the NFL. However, after suffering career-ending injuries and
mental health issues, his coaches forced him to step away from
the sport. When trying to figure out what was next, there was
nothing he wanted to do except continue football. He didn't
have his eyes set on anything else.

In his book, *Who Am I After Sports?* he recalls trying to find
new activities, but nothing was the same as football. He said,
"Football and basketball were my passions! Running fast,
jumping high, and making plays were my gifts! So, what do
you do when sports are your passion, but you can no longer
play? What do you do when your talent is athleticism, but
you're no longer an athlete?"

Darryll identified so closely with football, it felt like he was
losing a part of himself. Instead of seeing himself as a hard
worker or team player, he labeled himself as an "athlete" which
couldn't transfer after competition was over. "I realized something was wrong if I felt like a nobody just because of a career

change. I realized sports had become who I was versus what I did, and I could see that losing sports had somehow equated to losing myself," Darryll recalled.

He saw his only passion and talent as being an athlete. This isn't true, but it's what a lot of athletes might believe. Because athletes have spent years dedicating time to their sport they may forget or may ignore other interests and skills they have. "Then one day, I suddenly had a liberating thought. What if none of my passions were fulfilling because I wasn't as good at them as I was sports?" Darryll said. "It helped me realize that just because I didn't love anything more than sports didn't mean I couldn't love anything more than sports."

> Just because I didn't love anything more than sports didn't mean I couldn't love anything more than sports.

He realized that sports were fulfilling to him because he had dedicated so much time to practice and competing in football. It's not that athletes don't have any passions outside of athletics, it's just that they haven't practiced them yet. People will naturally be drawn to things that they're good at. Then, when they do pick up something new, they compare their beginner-level skills to the high status they had once achieved in sport. Just like it took many hours and years to become good at being an athlete, anything new in life will have to go through that same process.

Once Darryll had this realization he said, "I had forgotten what it was like to be a beginner and start from scratch. I had been so good at sports for so long that not being good at something was awkward." If an athlete approaches their new career, hobby, or skill they're trying to improve just like they approached sports, they'll realize there are other things they can become passionate in. Just like an athlete wouldn't go to their first practice and try out for a starting position, they shouldn't expect to naturally excel at the next thing they try after sports.

BEING A BEGINNER AGAIN:

Starting over as a beginner is tough. No one enjoys being at the bottom of the totem pole. Sometimes when having to make this change, athletes can also feel behind in life compared to their peers. Prioritizing athletics might have been at the sacrifice of getting job experience, building romantic relationships, or creating an income stream. To feel like you must learn everything new and to feel behind while doing so can be discouraging.

A big thing that helps athletes going through these growing pains is to focus on building a new identity. Studies show that people react to and interpret situations differently based on their current identity and prefer identity-congruent actions.

From the study *Identity-Based Motivation: Implications for Intervention* researchers found, "When action feels identity-congruent, experienced difficulty highlights that the behavior is important and meaningful. When action feels identity-incongruent, the same difficulty suggests that the behavior is pointless and 'not for people like me.'"

This means without a strong identity when facing difficulties, it's easier to call it quits and think it's not worth it. That it's not worth it to go to the gym every day since they're not training for a competition. That it's not worth it to try to excel at their job because they don't get the same recognition as an athletic competition. If a former athlete doesn't change their identity from competing athlete to everyday athlete, career-focused person, or any other identity, then tough situations will be harder to push through. If they have a tough day at work, the mindset could easily change to "well I'm not passionate about it anyways," instead of seeing the benefit of committing to finishing the work.

In the same study, researchers state, "Research is beginning to provide evidence that possible future identities can influence current action when the possible future identity feels connected to the current self, whether the possible identity describes a near or far future." So, even if an athlete doesn't know their next steps after retirement, just having a possible future identity can help. It might not happen immediately, but identifying as their next phase (as coach or graduate student, for example) can help feeling passion and purpose around their actions.

> Athletes have to put in work to be good at something again.

From Darryll's story, just like many others, athletes have to put in work to be good at something again. An athlete's new identity won't be one that they're great at right away. One of the ways a former athlete can begin to construct a future self is to build their life around habits that fit that self. Expert habit builder James Clear, author of *Atomic Habits,* also connects habits and identity. In his book, James says, "The key to building lasting habits is focusing on creating a new identity first. Your current behaviors are simply a reflection of your current identity. What you do now is a mirror image of the type of person you believe that you are (either consciously or subconsciously)." A person's identity is a huge factor in their motivation, how they act, and who they want to become. What is the next identity that you want to work towards?

STEP NINE. S - SPARK A NEW INTEREST:

Former athlete, here is your wake-up call: you are not just a former athlete. If you only refer to yourself in that way, even subconsciously, it's how you will act. But at this point you may think to yourself: What is my new identity? How do I know what to focus on?

James Clear addresses this too. He says, "Many people begin the process of changing their habits by focusing on *what* they want to achieve. This leads us to outcome-based habits. The alternative is to build identity-based habits. With this approach, we start by focusing on *who* we wish to become." To build a new identity, focus on what type of person you'd like to become. It's hard to ask yourself "what is my passion?" but if you focus on who you'd like to be and what interests you, it can help get you there. If you like art, build habits around creating art. If you enjoy trivia, is there a weekly club you can join? If there is a cause you're passionate about, try finding somewhere you can volunteer or an activity you can do to raise money. You can set aside some time each week to draw, volunteer, run, or whatever else excites you. Eventually, these habits build up over time and you practice more and more as the months go on.

After deciding what type of person you want to be, the steps and motivation to get there start to become more obvious. James says: "Changing your beliefs isn't nearly as hard as you might think. There are two steps. 1. Decide the type of person you want to be. 2. Prove it to yourself with small wins." Remember that you are still a beginner no matter how much something piques your interest. Take notice of any and all small wins that you come across while trying something new.

James also says, "If you're looking to make a change, then I say stop worrying about results and start worrying about your identity. Become the type of person who can achieve the things you want to achieve."

> Stop worrying about results and start worrying about your identity. Become the type of person who can achieve the things you want to achieve.

The great news is that athletes already know they can achieve great things! You've proven to yourself time and time again on the court, field, or anywhere else that you can push yourself past what you thought possible. Unexpected wins, new personal records, and just the sheer number of hours put into your sport have shown you what is possible to conquer. Time to take that same ambition to your new interest.

9 Steps to Getting Off the S.I.D.E.L.I.N.E.S. of Life

	THE NEW UNKNOWN	
S	Slow Down	☐
I	Intuitively Eat	☐
D	Develop Body Acceptance	☐
	THE MESSY MIDDLE	
E	Explore Your Identity	☐
L	Love Your Workout	☐
I	Improve Nutrition Knowledge	☐
	BETTER DAYS AHEAD	
N	Nurture New Athletic Role	☐
E	Expand Your Comfort Zone	☐
S	Spark a New Interest	☐

At this point, you have now learned the SIDELINES transition to go from Elite to Everyday Athlete. You are ready to start your next adventure knowing that you can build on what made you an athlete. The ball is now in your court. This isn't a brand-new chapter, it's a bridge into what's next.

* * *

To hear more about Darryll's journey out of the NFL and his new company, Second Chance Athletes, listen to our conversation on my podcast, *Live Your Personal Best*, at emilycoffman. org/darryllstinson

PHASE FOUR: EXTRA INNINGS

CHAPTER 10:

THE BALL IS IN YOUR COURT

———

"At some point in time, we cease to use the skills we learned but we always remember the words we heard."

—COACH REED, STAFF COACH FOR THE CINCINNATI
SAINTS PROFESSIONAL SOCCER TEAM

Athletes,

It's important to take charge of your own transition. While I already laid out the steps on how to get off the sidelines of life, there are a few more things worth noting for the smoothest transition possible.

PLAN AHEAD:

If possible, start thinking about the transition out of athletics before it happens. It'll be easier to transition if you're able to create an identity that's not centered around sports while you still have sports in your life. Stay active in your interests outside of sports as much as possible. Then, when you're no longer a competing athlete, you already have these habits and experiences to build on.

Athletes tend to start this process too late, because they wait until they're already retired before they think about life after sports. If it's still possible, take the extra time now to think about what your life will look like without sports. Ask yourself: What are some things outside of sports that you enjoy? What do you wish you could dedicate more time to? If you weren't doing sports, what would you be doing? Exploring these questions will give you an idea of other things in your life besides just sports.

BE A FOREVER TEAMMATE:

When talking with former athletes, the number one thing they wish they did more of was talking with their old teammates after competition was over. Former athletes recall feeling alone in this transition and this led them to isolate themselves further from their teammates. When you're going through this transition, you are never alone. You have your current teammates who are going through the transition with you, and other teammates who have already gone through this transition before. Just because they aren't talking about the mental, emotional, or physical toll leaving athletics has had on them does not mean they're not affected by it. These feelings are a lot more common than we often think.

> Your team isn't gone just because you're not wearing matching uniforms.

Just like they were your teammates while competing, they can still be your teammates in life. They can still be that support system for you, and they can still help you out with this next stage.

You come from the same background; you're going through different yet similar struggles. Your team isn't gone just because you're not wearing matching uniforms.

RELAX:

Remember to not take yourself so seriously. We get stuck in the constant win and lose in sports, but that's not how life is. Life isn't about winning and losing; there's not a winner and loser. If you stop seeing everything you do as something you need to be successful at and "win" compared to your peers, you will find it easier to be content with your current position.

These steps in this book can help get you to a place of being healthy and happy, but this isn't meant to be your next rule-book to follow. There is no rulebook or playbook of life. Stop thinking of your life as the next tournament you need to win. Check in with yourself and assess, "Do I have things in my life I enjoy?" If yes, that's awesome, keep enjoying those and don't feel the need to become the best at it. If no, take steps to see how you can start adding things in your life that you do enjoy. This should not be something that you're necessarily good at or something that can be competitive, but something that will add happiness to your life. Don't take yourself so seriously and think that you have to take down your "competition." There is no such thing as the champion of life.

* * *

Parents,

Your support is needed now more than ever. Since your athlete's other support system and community disappears after sports, you might be the one stable support in their life. There are a few ways you could best help your athlete.

BE A PARENT:

If you have an athlete going through this transition, you must establish yourself outside of being their fan. It's great for an athlete when their parent can be their biggest cheerleader, come to all their competitions, and be cheering them on every step of the way. But if a parent's support drops off when sports do, it can make an athlete seem like sports was the only thing interesting about them, or that they were the reason that you were supporting them. It's time to go from their cheerleader to their parent again.

> It's time to go from their cheerleader to their parent again.

When I was competing, I remember my parents came to every race, every single weekend of competition season, and they wouldn't miss these for the world. But once I stopped competing and I moved closer to home, I didn't see them as much. They no longer had to travel all over the country. They only had to drive down the street. We weren't given the excuse of a race, and we weren't placing the same emphasis on family dinner. When you're going through so much change, having a constant, like a parent's support in your life, is crucial. Even if sports were easier to follow, keep checking in with the new activities in your athlete's life. Check in about their new job, new school, or even just ask how they're doing. This will give them the reassurance that there's more to them than their sport.

REMIND THEM:

Another way to support your athlete is by reminding them who they were outside of their sport. Athletes have often been competing for so long, since elementary or middle school, that they might have forgotten who they were without sports. Remind them of the communities that they were a part of, other parts of their identity, or other interests that they had. Before your athlete had dreams of being an athlete, did they have dreams of being anything else? What other activities did they try? As a parent, you probably remember it better than they do. Instead of only bringing up the past as it relates to them being a great athlete and their sports accomplishments, remind them of things outside of who they were as an athlete.

Sarah Stokowski, a PhD student in college athlete development, wrote in an article for AthleticDirectorU, "Parents can be an incredible ally in promoting a holistic student-athlete identity simply by making sure student-athletes know that their parents' value and support them beyond what they do on the field or the court." Let them know what they're feeling is valid and that they are more than just an athlete. They aren't a one-hit wonder, and they will find another thing to be passionate about after sports end.

GUIDE THEM:

As a parent, you don't need to be an expert here. Just like when your kid started athletics, you signed them up for their first team. You didn't coach them through learning the sport, just pointed them in the right direction, and the coach did the rest. You can do that again now. You can recommend resources for them. You can refer them to other people. You should give them a copy of this book if they haven't read it already.

You should recommend podcasts like *Live Your Personal Best* which helps with workout motivation and living a healthy lifestyle. There are resources out there for them you can pass along. Gently guide them in the right direction when they're at this crossroad. Your athlete might not be equipped for the transition, and you might not be either, but there are plenty of psychologists, nutritionists, trainers, counselors, and more who can help.

On the other hand, don't try to "fix" this for them. There's nothing that will fix their feelings, just different ways to cope with them. It can be hard to see your athlete struggle with this adjustment, but your support will help more than an attempt at pushing the problem away.

* * *

Coaches,

During an athlete's career, they have looked to you for guidance and direction. From your perspective, while it may look that it's just in athletics, this is something that affects all aspects of their life. Your support and guidance don't stop at the edge of the playing field. I talked to my old college coach, John Gartin, about how coaches can help with this transition. He was a rowing coach for over ten years and is now the director of career development at Northern Arizona University. He has spent years guiding athletes to their next stage of life and has a few recommendations on how coaches can help support transitioning athletes.

BRIDGE THE GAP:

Reassure your athlete that just because they're starting a new chapter doesn't mean that they're starting completely new. They can bridge who they were in athletics into the next phase of their life. They're done being an athlete but that's it. Does that mean they're done being a leader? Done being a great teammate?

"What we need to do is go we're going to teach you all these skills to be a captain on a team. And now we're going to show you how that matters. In all of these aspects of work, life, volunteerism, you name it, here's the bridge," explains Coach Gartin. "So, not only are you learning all of these things on how to be a better team captain, also all the stuff that the employers are looking for. And then for that to be intentional and making that bridge. Again, we have to teach them to construct each bridge."

Your role as the coach can be to show them how the skills they're already using matter outside of sports. When leaving competition, it's not starting new, it's bridging a gap from where they currently are to where they're going. Coach Gartin recommends that coaches explicitly help athletes understand how their skills matter. He says, "We need to teach them to be able to understand that. The problem is there's a mistaken assumption that the athlete gets it, and the athlete knows the lesson, even when we haven't taught it."

COMMUNICATION:

Don't let the transition be an untouched subject. The end of their career is

> There's a mistaken assumption that the athlete gets it, and the athlete knows the lesson, even when we haven't taught it.

inevitable at some point, so it's important to not look at it as a taboo subject. Talking about what an athlete will do after sports doesn't mean that the athlete is less committed to the sport, just that they're looked at as a more well-rounded person.

Talking with coaches about life outside of athletics can sometimes feel like a taboo subject. As their coach, initiate having a conversation about what their life looks like after sport. Talk to them about their life outside of sports, what their plan is after competition is over, and other interests in their life to acknowledge them as a person, not just an athlete.

Coaches do a good job preparing athletes to continue competing at a higher level, but many athletes never go to a further level. Often a coach is training them to be a member of their team and then the athlete will retire onto something new. Coach Gartin states that this is part of the coach's job. "A coach's job is to prepare you for the next step and for many people higher competition isn't the next step."

Talk to your athletes and help plug them into the programs available to them. Can you put them in touch with career resources? Study abroad? Volunteering? Any dedicated service to former athletes? By talking to athletes about these services, you're conveying to them the importance of being a well-versed student-athlete.

STAY CONNECTED:

Create a space where an athlete can still stay connected. Let them know that just because they aren't competing doesn't mean they aren't part of the team. For home competitions, have an alumnus pregame or watch area. Send them a Christmas card the first year after graduation. Connect them with another former athlete that could act as a mentor. Create a natural opportunity for them to reach out to you if they need to.

Will Ruth, a strength coach, wrote an article about how he helps former athletes stay connected. He said, "I made a tradition of hosting a 'senior lift' event for graduating athletes. This gave athletes something to look forward to after racing concluded, introduced one element of post-transition physical activity, and provided a natural opportunity for further discussion on transitioning from sport."

Athletes don't want to feel kicked out of the team just because they're not competing anymore. The team and coaches may still be like family to them, and an environment where they feel comfortable. Coach Gartin summarizes by saying, "Once you've coached that person, they're on your team, period." Small efforts of staying connected after sports can make the world of difference to someone struggling through this transition.

* * *

Just like it took a village to build up a competitive athlete, the team will still be there when moving on to the next stage. They supported you for the person you were and will continue doing so in your next phase. Everyone's roles might look a little different, but the support is still there. Don't shut the door behind you when leaving this chapter of your life.

EPILOGUE

———

"You can't make the hard right decisions today without faith in tomorrow."

—RORY VADEN, AUTHOR OF TAKE THE STAIRS

———————————————————

The truth is, it's hard to replace everything that athletics was. This realization came to me over a year after my last race. I was so focused on applying for jobs, moving to a new city, and enjoying the things I had been missing out on that the first year seemed like a blur. But after the excitement of a new life started to become mundane again, I looked around at my new life. I wasn't moving forward. I was just stuck.

What I did, and what so many former athletes do, was blindly follow back into society's expectations. I got a job and fully dove in, working all hours of the clock to improve my skills just so I didn't have to be a beginner again. But athletes have never fully followed a traditional path. We're used to paving our own way. We've made school, sports, and jobs fit together while still saving enough time to recover and sometimes relax.

We've thought outside the box on how to beat opponents and climb out of being the underdog. Now is no different. If you put in the work, you will see success in your transition. There will be no more looking at the past thinking, "Those were the glory days." I want you to look back and think, "Look at all that I accomplished, and what it's helping me accomplish next." The goal isn't over, the game has just changed.

* * *

Former Olympian Melinda Harrison said, "Anyone who strives for a personal best will face a personal next."

* * *

Every athlete goes through a period of transition, from elite to everyday athlete, and will find their personal next. The first step, and one of the most important, is to prioritize your needs. Then, as you feel excitement for the new unknown, practice incorporating rest, listening to your body, and changing your body perception so you can hit the ground running once your sport is over. When things turn into the messy middle, set yourself up for a great third period by separating who you are from what you do, finding fitness that fits your lifestyle, and breaking the rules you had as an athlete. Lastly, when you feel stuck, you can find that personal next by finding ways to keep sports in your life, going outside your comfort zone, and identifying a future goal.

So, what does my life look like now? I found a healthy balance between taking care of my body and prioritizing things outside of the gym. I haven't created one new identity, but many. I have a full-time career for which I studied in college. I host a top health and fitness podcast, *Live Your Personal Best*, and, most recently, I became an author. I have a good relationship with food, my body, and have a supportive new community around me. I am happy living the life of an everyday athlete.

By following the steps from this book, you can walk into life after sports with a plan that will make the next stage of your life just as good, if not better, than wherever you're at now. Your past doesn't determine where you go, it helps determine how you grow. My hope is that you get off the sidelines of life and go for the gold.

* * *

A full list of all resources mentioned in this book can be found at emilycoffman.org

READER'S GUIDE

———

Below you'll find discussion questions and action steps to help you implement these lessons into your daily life. Use these questions as journal prompts, self-reflections, or discussion starters with teammates. I hope this guide helps you have a smoother transition and gives you more confidence during this next phase on how to become an everyday athlete.

KICKED OUT OF THE NEST

1. What "loss" was the hardest? Were you able to find any replacements for it outside of athletics?

2. What did the end of your athletic career look like? How has that affected your outlook on your whole career?

3. What feelings have come up for you after leaving sports?

Action: After putting your team and sport first for so long, it's time to prioritize yourself. Pay attention to what you need and put your needs first!

S - SLOW DOWN

1. What does your relationship with rest look like? How can it be improved?

2. What is your routine when you feel most rested?

3. How can you find a healthy balance between activity and rest? How will you prioritize that balance?

Action: Retirement is the same as a never-ending off-season. You need to slow down and incorporate rest regularly to feel rejuvenated.

I - INTUITIVELY EAT

1. What does a typical day of eating look like for you? What is this motivated by?

2. How would becoming more aware of your hunger and fullness cues change the way you're eating?

3. Do you hope to get more or less strict with your eating after athletics? How do you feel intuitive eating would work for you?

Action: Start intuitively eating by listening to your hunger cues. Your body will naturally adapt to your changed routine and habits. You just have to listen.

D - DEVELOP BODY ACCEPTANCE

1. How do you feel about your body? Are these things really true?

2. What is your reaction to your body changes?

3. How can you celebrate your body? How is this view different from the way you have thought in the past?

Action: Develop body acceptance by acknowledging that change isn't bad, and accept your body changes. Your body's appearance does not affect your worth.

E – EXPLORE YOUR IDENTITY

4. What part of your athletic identity did you love most? How can you bring that into a new area of your life?

5. What's preventing you from expanding past your athlete identity?

6. Who would you be if you didn't pursue your sport?

Action: Separate who you are from what you do. Explore who you are when you aren't defined by your work.

L – LOVE YOUR WORKOUT

1. How would you describe your current workout routine? Is it something you're happy with?

2. What are your intentions with your new workouts? Do you have a specific goal, or do you just enjoy staying active?

3. How has your mindset around working out changed now that you're not competing?

Action: Your workouts and training schedule will look different from what you followed while competing. Find fitness that fits your lifestyle.

I – IMPROVE NUTRITION KNOWLEDGE

1. What are some nutrition guidelines that you follow? Look back and evaluate. Are they rooted in nutrition or rules?

2. Where have you learned about food and how to eat it? Do you trust that source?

3. What motivation do you have to live a healthier lifestyle?

Action: Knowledge relaxes rules. Learn more about basic nutrition and old food rules will become less important.

N - NURTURE A NEW ATHLETIC ROLE

1. How do you see sports and your new athletic identity show up in your life?

2. How has taking on a new athletic role changed how you view sports? How does it feel to participate from a different perspective?

3. In your opinion what does it mean to be an everyday athlete?

Action: Lack of competition does not mean a lack of athletic identity. Find new ways to keep sports in your life.

E - EXPAND YOUR COMFORT ZONE

1. What are you most excited to try next? On the other hand, what are you most nervous about or what scares you?

2. Where are you getting the most fulfillment from right now?

3. Think about all the times you had to step out of your comfort zone in sports. What advice do you give yourself?

Action: To find new passions you have to try new things. Get uncomfortable and go outside your comfort zone.

S - SPARK A NEW INTEREST

1. Which step of the transition was the hardest for you to work through? Why?

2. How does it feel to be a beginner again? What can you learn from the last time you were a beginner?

3. What is the biggest thing you've learned about yourself through this transition?

Action: Stop looking to the past, and start planning for the future. Find new interests and identify a future goal to work towards.

* * *

Download a printable copy of the reader's guide at:
http://emilycoffman.org/bookresources

ACKNOWLEDGEMENTS

There are many people without whom this book wouldn't have been possible, and I am grateful to all of them. My readers, there would be no book without you.

Cathy & Howie Coffman - Without you both, there would be no sports career to write about. Thank you for being the best cheerleaders and parents.

Linda & Michael Curley - Thank you for being there through every transition and supporting every venture I try.

Matthew Gately - Thank you for spending countless hours helping me write this book. I don't know if anyone else will ever read it as many times as you have.

Alyssa Hance - Thank you for your valuable insights that made this book into what it is today.

Haley Perry & Victoria Lasin - Thank you for being generous with your words of encouragement.

Thank you to the athletes and coaches who took time out of their day to discuss ideas for this book and share their journeys. Your stories are what made this possible:

Taylor Spencer, John Gartin, Rich Chapman, Brenna Dowell, Melissa "Twist" Patten, Chloé Campbell, Abby Lange, Nina Chism, Julianne O'Connell, Bethany Hart Gerry, Elena Sturdivant, Steve Vanderberg, Millicent Sykes, Sarah Rapaport, Ashley Alveraz, Katherine Kuhlman, Alex Klein, Kelly Garrison Funderburk, Kaitlyn Daugherty, Mitch Greene, and Ingrid Marcum.

Thank you to the people who believed in this book before it was even fully complete. Without your belief in me, this book would not have been able to be created:

Charles Coffman, Lauren McAndrew, Joseph E. Hunt IV, Cameron Robison, Rachael Berthiaume, AnnMarie Stowe, Emily Taylor, Alexa Freitas, Sarah Nitenson, Kristin Frongillo, Tracey Faraday, Audrey Kilgore, Brittany Baine, Whitney Chandler, Reagan Collins, Ankita Sinha, Gina McAndrew, Toni-Ann Mayembe, Mariel Wade, Maddie Adelman, Marjorie Young, Jill Craighead, Savannah Rose Cloar, Debra Sharon, Carly Railing, Shawna Scafe, Deborah Kublin, Natalie Brown, Amy Johnson, Rob Coffman, Jennifer Logan, Kris Stapleton, Zack McIntyre, Michelle Kasteard, Sydney Umeri, Katherine Costello, Miriam Coffman, Josh Williams, Rubie Blanchard, Miranda Rauner, Amy Adamczyk, Rachel Williams, Liz Siracusa, Carlos Moran, Martha Gately, Cory Camp, Baylee Barnes, Jennifer Franklin, Bentleigh Albert, Katie Quinn, Alex Sullivan, Teri Akuk, Jazmine Highsmith, Alexandra Rosenthal, Ethan Delaney, Debbie Truax, Hope Johnston, Kelsey Buehler, Carol Holtan, Kayla Friesen, Sarah Thomashower, Mike Squires, John Fuchs, Hannah Biffle, Hannah Kloppenburg, Ethan Forman, Danica Durdines, Alexa Walsh, Sarah McAndrews, Janette Coleman, Sarah Segner, Kenzie Campbell, Sydney Holgado, Torry Dugan,

Belle Stixrood, Ashley Carpenter, Louise Kuehster, Caleb Alemany, Aimee Shaye, Madison Hopkins, Jackie Sanderson, Andy Rodriguez-Sanchez, Jason Keller, Aaron Rogers, Amy Hance, Amy Young, Neelie Kibler, Natalie Grimes, Eva Meier, Lauren Bracken, Dr. Michael Coleman, Katie Bruggeling, Erin Nicholson, Cynthia Legelis, Natalie Justus, Shiann Gardner, Jordan Norris, Sarita Biswas, András Nemeth, Jason Truax, Katie Rash, Dustin Bingham, Emily Erdman, Brooke Engles, Amanda Pearson, Cindy Gilbert

Lastly, I want to thank the people who helped me accomplish this dream of mine and turn my rambling stories into a published book:

Professor Eric Koester, Editors Cody Heining and Sandy Huffman, and Coach Rory Vaden.

APPENDIX

EPIGRAPH

Rapkin, Brett, dir.*The Weight of Gold*. HBO Max, 2020. https://www.hbo.com/documentaries/the-weight-of-gold.

INTRODUCTION

Cleveland Clinic. "How to Break Bad Habits." Health Essentials from Cleveland Clinic, December 8, 2020. https://health.clevelandclinic.org/how-to-break-bad-habits/.

McLaughlin, Kelly. "Aly Raisman Confirms She Won't Compete in the 2020 Tokyo Olympics in an Emotional Letter on Instagram." Business Insider. Business Insider, January 16, 2020. https://www.businessinsider.com/aly-raisman-confirmed-retirement-tokyo-2020-olympics-instagram-2020-1.

National Eating Disorders Association. "Statistics & Research on Eating Disorders." May 8, 2020. https://www.nationaleatingdisorders.org/statistics-research-eating-disorders.

Sorenson, Shawn C. "Couch Potato Athletes: Why It's Hard to Stay Active after Competition Ends." The Washington Post.

WP Company, July 25, 2014. https://www.washingtonpost.
com/opinions/couch-potato-athletes-why-its-hard-to-stay-
active-after-competition-ends/2014/07/25/19fc0144-0b6d-11e4-
8c9a-923eccoc7d23_story.html.

HAPTER ONE - THE NEXT HURDLE

Adams, Steve. "Dustin Pedroia Announces Retirement."
MLB Trade Rumors, February 1, 2021. https://www.
mlbtraderumors.com/2021/02/dustin-pedroia-retirement.
html#comments.

Athletes Soul. "Richie Crowley: Former Bostonian Professional
Hockey Player Turned Cultured Creative Director." Accessed
January 12, 2021. https://www.athletessoul.space/richie-
crowley.html.

Harrison, Melinda. *Personal Next: What We Can Learn from Elite
Athletes Navigating Career Transition.* Vancouver, Canada:
LifeTree Media, 2020.

Weinberg, Robert S., and Daniel Gould. "Enhancing Health and
Well-Being." Essay. In *Foundations of Sport and Exercise
Psychology,* Fifthed., 399. Champaign, IL: Human Kinetics, 2011.

Wertheim, Jon. "Inside the Life of the Modern pro Athlete in
Retirement." Sports Illustrated. Sports Illustrated, July 3,
2017. https://www.si.com/nba/2017/07/03/retired-athletes-life-
money-health#gid=ci02553872d0042580&pid=duane-starks.

CHAPTER TWO - THE NEVER-ENDING OFF SEASON

Agostino, Jill. "Once an Athletic Star, Now an Unheavenly
Body." The New York Times. The New York Times,
July 6, 2006. https://www.nytimes.com/2006/07/06/
fashion/06Fitness.html?pagewanted=all.

Garrick, Victoria. "From Division I Athlete to Retired Athlete... Finding My New Fitness Routine!" YouTube. YouTube, August 20, 2020. https://www.youtube.com/watch?v=audXKcZQx_Q.

Lemonick, Hillary. "I Was Burned Out on Fitness-Until I Found Peloton." The Output, October 22, 2020. https://blog.onepeloton.com/student-athlete-peloton/.

Sorenson, Shawn C., Russell Romano, Stanley P. Azen, E. Todd Schroeder, and George J. Salem. "Life Span Exercise Among Elite Intercollegiate Student Athletes." Sports Health 7, no. 1 (January 2015): 80–86. https://doi.org/10.1177/1941738114534813.

Underhill, Allison. "The Former Athlete's Guide to Staying in Shape." US News & World Report. US News & World Report, July 15, 2016. https://health.usnews.com/wellness/articles/2016-07-15/the-former-athletes-guide-to-staying-in-shape.

Weinberg, Robert S., and Daniel Gould. "Enhancing Health and Well-Being." Essay. In *Foundations of Sport and Exercise Psychology*, Fifth ed., 399. Champaign, IL: Human Kinetics, 2011.

CHAPTER THREE - FUELING YOUR LIFESTYLE

Associated Press. "Jockeys Still Dealing with Weight Issues." Los Angeles Times. Los Angeles Times, April 27, 2008. https://www.latimes.com/archives/la-xpm-2008-apr-27-sp-jockeys27-story.html.

Crouch, Bethany. Intuitive Eating & Navigating Nutrition After Sport with Bri Collette. Other. *Your Sports Story*, June 26, 2019. https://podcasts.apple.com/us/podcast/your-sport-story/id1449065990.

Crouch, Bethany. Owning Your Health On The Run with Former Basketball Athlete, Kelsey Anselmi. Other. *Your Sport Story*,

May 11, 2019. https://podcasts.apple.com/us/podcast/your-sport-story/id1449065990?i=1000437846232.

Maffetone, Philip B., and Paul B. Laursen. "Athletes: Fit but Unhealthy?" Sports Medicine - Open. US National Library of Medicine, May 26, 2016. https://www.ncbi.nlm.nih.gov/pmc/articles/PMC4882373/.

"Retired Athletes Are Fighting Fat." The Washington Times. The Washington Times, April 23, 2001. https://www.washingtontimes.com/news/2001/apr/23/20010423-022122-3981r/.

Tribole, Evelyn, and Elyse Resch. "Honor Your Hunger." Essay. In *Intuitive Eating: a Revolutionary Anti-Diet Approach*, 4th ed., 84–95. New York, NY: St. Martin's Essentials, 2020.

CHAPTER FOUR - EMBRACING THE CHANGES

Anxiety and Depression Association of America, ADAA. "Body Dysmorphic Disorder (BDD)." Accessed January 31, 2021. https://adaa.org/understanding-anxiety/related-illnesses/other-related-conditions/body-dysmorphic-disorder-bdd.

Buckley, Georgina L et al. "Retired Athletes and the Intersection of Food and Body: A Systematic Literature Review Exploring Compensatory Behaviours and Body Change." Nutrients vol. 11,6 1395. 21 Jun. 2019, doi:10.3390/nu11061395.

Griffiths, Scott. "Body Acceptance." Encyclopedia of Personality and Individual Differences. Springer Link, February 22, 2017. https://link.springer.com/referenceworkentry/10.1007%2F978-3-319-28099-8_486-1.

Kale, Sirin. "Gym, Eat, Repeat: the Shocking Rise of Muscle Dysmorphia." The Guardian. Guardian News and Media, July 17, 2019. https://www.theguardian.com/lifeandstyle/2019/

jul/17/gym-eat-repeat-the-shocking-rise-of-muscle-dysmorphia.

Laure, Caroline E., and Nichole Meline. 2018. "Examining Body Image in Retired Collegiate Volleyball Players". *Journal of Kinesiology & Wellness* 7 (1), 29-45. https://www.wskw.org/jkw/index.php/jkw/article/view/8.

TrueSport. "Why Do Some Athletes Struggle with Body Image?" Team USA, June 24, 2020. https://www.teamusa.org/USA-Field-Hockey/Features/2020/June/24/Why-do-Some-Athletes-Struggle-with-Body-Image.

CHAPTER FIVE - THE INNER ATHLETE

Buckley, Georgina L et al. "Retired Athletes and the Intersection of Food and Body: A Systematic Literature Review Exploring Compensatory Behaviours and Body Change." *Nutrients* vol. 11,6 1395. 21 Jun. 2019, doi:10.3390/nu11061395

Costa, Phil, and Rob Curley. *The Transition Playbook for ATHLETES*, 2019.

Davis, Jeffrey. "You Are Not Your Work." Psychology Today. Sussex Publishers, March 26, 2019. https://www.psychologytoday.com/us/blog/tracking-wonder/201903/you-are-not-your-work.

Disanjh, Jordan. "⊠The Transparently Jordan Podcast: 3x Olympic Gold Medalist Stephanie Rice on What Is Life Like After Winning 3 Olympic Gold Medals, The Importance of Reflection, Working to Be Better & More." Apple Podcasts, October 5, 2020. https://podcasts.apple.com/us/podcast/3x-olympic-gold-medalist-stephanie-rice-on-what-is/id1508636687?i=1000493690588.

Garrick, Victoria. "⊠Real Pod: The Max Browne Interview - What Really Happened to the Nation's #1

Recruit on Apple Podcasts." Apple Podcasts, May 20, 2020. https://podcasts.apple.com/us/podcast/real-pod/id1466166364?i=1000475182942.

Link, Lauren. *Healthy Former Athlete: Nutrition and Fitness Advice for the Transition from Elite Athlete to Normal Human.* Skyhorse Publishing Company, 2018.

NCAA Research. "Estimated Probability of Competing in Professional Athletics." NCAA.org - The Official Site of the NCAA, April 20, 2020. https://www.ncaa.org/about/resources/research/estimated-probability-competing-professional-athletics.

Pattison, Claudette Montana. "Where Are They Now: Max Browne Talks Sam Darnold & Kedon Slovis." Sports Illustrated USC Trojans News, Analysis and More. Sports Illustrated USC Trojans News, Analysis and More, November 1, 2020. https://www.si.com/college/usc/football/where-are-they-now-max-browne-talks-usc.

CHAPTER SIX - LACING UP

"Anja Garcia: Fitness Trainer by Day, Nurse by Night." Athletes Soul. Accessed February 4, 2021. https://www.athletessoul.space/anja-garcia.html.

Athletes Soul. "Rebecca Soni: Six-Time Olympic Medalist Now Mentoring Young Athletes." Accessed February 4, 2021. https://www.athletessoul.space/rebecca-soni.html.

Cleveland Clinic. "How to Shift From Being an Athlete to an Active Adult." Health Essentials from Cleveland Clinic, December 24, 2020. https://health.clevelandclinic.org/transitioning-from-athlete-to-active-adult/.

Palmer, Whitney J. "KINESIOLOGY RESEARCH FOCUSES ON KEEPING STUDENT-ATHLETES HEALTHY AFTER

GRADUATION." UNCG NEWS. UNC Greensboro, March
20, 2018. https://news.uncg.edu/kinesiology-research-
keeping-student-athletes-healthy/?fbclid=IwAR1bpU3kBJrwG
f8z9gibs-dxdyoOLn8AYof6_tL9wQRPgdm3n4sIBZmZD7Y.

Smith, Chris. "Why Is It So Hard For Athletes To Feel
Successful?" Athlete Network. Accessed May 31, 2021. https://
an.athletenetwork.com/blog/why-is-it-so-hard-for-athletes-
to-feel-successful.

CHAPTER SEVEN - BREAKING FOOD RULES

Hargrave, Katie. *The Athlete After: a 10-Week Guide to Balancing
Life After Sports*. CreateSpace Independent Publishing
Platform, 2016.

Jackson, Nicola. "Why You Can Break up with Food Rules."
Healthy Food Guide. Healthy Food Guide, March 17,
2021. https://www.healthyfood.com/advice/why-you-should-
break-up-with-food-rules/.

Nail Your Nutrition. "Nail Your Nutrition Podcast: How
Disordered Eating Affects Current and Former Athletes of All
Levels with Georgie Buckley, Dietitian and PhD Candidate
on Apple Podcasts." Apple Podcasts, August 17, 2020. https://
podcasts.apple.com/us/podcast/nail-your-nutrition-podcast/
id1509794930?i=1000488528090.

National Eating Disorders Association. "Athletes &
Eating Disorders." April 18, 2019. https://www.
nationaleatingdisorders.org/athletes-eating-disorders.

Orenstein, Beth W. "How Fit Are You?: A Fitness Test for Adults
- Fitness - Everyday Health." EverydayHealth.com, June 14,
2012. https://www.everydayhealth.com/fitness/how-fit-are-
you-a-fitness-test-for-adults.aspx

World Health Organization. "Frequently Asked Questions."
Accessed May 31, 2021. https://www.who.int/about/who-we-
are/frequently-asked-questions.

CHAPTER EIGHT - BE A CAMO

Athletes Transitions. "Mentorship and Building a Network."
Accessed May 31, 2021. https://athletetransitions.ca/
mentorship-and-building-a-network.

Franken, Robert E., and Douglas J. Brown. "Why Do People like
Competition? The Motivation for Winning, Putting Forth
Effort, Improving One's Performance, Performing Well,
Being Instrumental, and Expressing Forceful/Aggressive
Behavior." Personality and Individual Differences. Pergamon,
January 13, 2000. https://www.sciencedirect.com/science/
article/abs/pii/0191886995000355.

Goldschmidt, Grant. "The 9 Purposes of Being a Sports
Coach." eta College - Sport and Fitness College, August 15,
2019. https://www.etacollege.com/the-9-purposes-of-being-a-
sports-coach/.

GOLF.com. "GOLF's Subpar: Tony Romo Interview: Filling the
Void Left from Football with Golf, How Much He Actually
Practices, and His Career Goals on Apple Podcasts." Apple
Podcasts, October 20, 2020. https://podcasts.apple.com/us/
podcast/tony-romo-interview-filling-void-left-from-football/
id1498625027?i=1000495496666.

Mahoney, Brian. "Steve Nash Eager to Get Started on New
Career as Nets Coach." NBA.com. NBA.com, October 10,
2020. https://www.nba.com/news/steve-nash-eager-new-
career-nets-coach.

Reynolds, Gretchen. "Learning a New Sport May Be Good for the
Brain." The New York Times. The New York Times, March 2,

2016. https://well.blogs.nytimes.com/2016/03/02/learning-a-new-sport-may-be-good-for-the-brain/.

Simons, Eric. "What Science Can Tell Sportswriters about Why We Love Sports." Columbia Journalism Review, September 2014. https://archives.cjr.org/full_court_press/science_sportswriting.php.

CHAPTER NINE- BROADENING YOUR PLAYBOOK

Green, Sarah. "Escape Your Comfort Zone." Harvard Business Review, February 9, 2017. https://hbr.org/podcast/2017/02/escape-your-comfort-zone.

Livni, Ephrat. "A New Study from Yale Scientists Shows How Uncertainty Helps Us Learn." Quartz. Quartz, July 31, 2018. https://qz.com/1343503/a-new-study-from-yale-scientists-shows-how-uncertainty-helps-us-learn/.

Pink, Daniel H. *Drive: The Surprising Truth About What Motivates Us.* New York, NY: Penguin Group, 2009.

Schoenfeld, Bruce. "Drew Bledsoe on Brady, Barolos and Life after the NFL." ESPN. ESPN Internet Ventures, February 9, 2020. https://www.espn.com/nfl/story/_/id/28549696/drew-bledsoe-brady-barolos-life-nfl.

Seligman, Martin. "Authentic Happiness." University of Pennsylvania, April 2011. https://www.authentichappiness.sas.upenn.edu/learn/wellbeing.

Tennant, Kelli. *The Transition.* United States: CreateSpace Independent Publishing Platform, 2014.

YaleNew. "Aren't Sure? Brain Is Primed for Learning." July 19, 2018. https://news.yale.edu/2018/07/19/arent-sure-brain-primed-learning.

Yang, Nicole. "Drew Bledsoe Shares How Making Wine Is a Natural Extension of Football." Boston.com. The Boston Globe, February 26, 2018. https://www.boston.com/sports/new-england-patriots/2018/02/26/drew-bledsoe-doubleback-winery-vineyards.

Zilca, Ran. "Comfort Kills." Psychology Today. Sussex Publishers, January 27, 2011. https://www.psychologytoday.com/us/blog/confessions-techie/201101/comfort-kills.

CHAPTER TEN – PLAYING THE GAME OF LIFE

Clear, James. "Identity-Based Habits: How to Actually Stick to Your Goals This Year." James Clear, February 4, 2020. https://jamesclear.com/identity-based-habits.

Complex News. "Kendrick & Kobe Talk About Their Evolution to Greatness at ComplexCon 2017." Youtube. November 6, 2017. https://www.youtube.com/watch?v=TZE6YRDPpc8&feature=emb_logo.

Oyserman, Daphna, and Mesmin Destin. "Identity-Based Motivation: Implications for Intervention." The Counseling psychologist. US National Library of Medicine, October 2010. https://www.ncbi.nlm.nih.gov/pmc/articles/PMC3079278/.

Smith, Chris. "Why Is It So Hard For Athletes To Feel Successful?" Athlete Network. Accessed June 27, 2021. https://an.athletenetwork.com/blog/why-is-it-so-hard-for-athletes-to-feel-successful.

Stinson, Darryll. *Who Am I After Sports?: An Athlete's Roadmap to Discover New Purpose and Live Fulfilled*. S.l.: AUTHOR ACADEMY ELITE, 2020.

CHAPTER ELEVEN - THE BALL IS IN YOUR COURT

Maltbie, Coach Reed. *"Echoes beyond the Game: the Lasting Power of a Coach's Words | Coach Reed | TEDxCincinnati."* Filmed July 2015 in Cincinnati, OH. Tedx Talks YouTube. https://www.youtube.com/watch?v=EhRXQsoK6ls

Ruth, Will. "Athlete Transitioning from Sport." Rowing Stronger, May 23, 2016. https://rowingstronger.com/2016/05/23/athlete-transitioning-from-sport/.

Stokowski, Sarah. "Who Am I Without My Sport? Addressing Student-Athlete Transitions." Athletic Director U. https://www.athleticdirectoru.com/, October 15, 2019. https://www.athleticdirectoru.com/articles/student-athlete-transitions/.

EPILOGUE

Harrison, Melinda. *Personal next: What We Can Learn From Elite Athletes Navigating Career Transition.* Vancouver, Canada: LifeTree Media, 2020.

Vaden, Rory. *Take the Stairs: 7 Steps to Achieving True Success.* New York, NY: Perigee, 2013.

Made in the USA
Monee, IL
18 August 2022

11860808R00095